Remembering China 1935–1945

Bea Liu in 1947 during her visit home
from China.

Remembering China
1935-1945

A Memoir by
Bea Exner Liu

Minnesota Voices Project Number 76

NEW RIVERS PRESS 1996

Edited by C. W. Truesdale
Editorial Assistance by Carol Rutz
Book design by Richard Krogstad
Typesetting by Peregrine Graphics Services

The cover painting, "Conversations in Autumn," is used by permission of the
Cleveland Art Museum.

New Rivers Press is a non-profit literary press dedicated to publishing the very
best emerging writers in our region, nation, and world.

The publication of *Remembering China* has been made possible by generous
grants from Target Stores, Dayton's and Mervyn's by the Dayton Hudson Foundation, the Jerome Foundation, the Metropolitan Regional Arts Council (from
an appropriation by the Minnesota Legislature), the National Endowment for the
Arts, the North Dakota Council on the Arts, the South Dakota Arts Council, and
the James R. Thorpe Foundation.

Additional support has been provided by the Elmer Anderson Foundation, Bush
Foundation, General Mills Foundation, Liberty State Bank, the McKnight Foun-
dation, the Minnesota State Arts Board (through an appropriation by the Min-
nesota Legislature), the Star Tribune/Cowles Media Company, the Tennant
Company Foundation, and the contributing members of New Rivers Press.
New Rivers is a member agency of United Arts.

UNITED ARTS

NORTH DAKOTA COUNCIL
ON THE ARTS

SOUTH DAKOTA ARTS COUNCIL

NATIONAL
ENDOWMENT
FOR THE
ARTS

Remembering China has been manufactured in the United States of America for
New Rivers Press, 420 North 5th Street, Minneapolis, MN 55401. First Edition.

To my brother, Frank M. Exner,
who paved the way for me to
go to China, and saved my letters,
without which this book could
not have been written.

CONTENTS

FOREWORD

Several years ago my older brother gave me a thick file of the letters I had written from China to my family. I was amazed to find how much of the flavor of the times I had recorded. Somewhere among my things I had several notebooks which had been my journals off and on during the war. I also had several chapters of a book I had started to write while I was back in America in 1946. I had abandoned the project when it seemed that the public's appetite for war books had been sated.

In 1992 I wrote a novel about civilian life in China during the war with Japan, but bookseller friends told me it would be hard to market a first novel of that nature at that time. They said if I would write a memoir it would surely sell.

Thinking it over, I knew that I had ample sources for a memoir. The things written at the time had a sense of immediacy that I could never duplicate from a perspective of fifty years. With selections from the letters, the journals, and the 1946 manuscript I would need only a small amount of retrospective material to make the connections. This book is the result—the story of my own experiences in the wartime conditions as they developed, and by implication the story of what the war meant to the Chinese people, especially academic types like us.

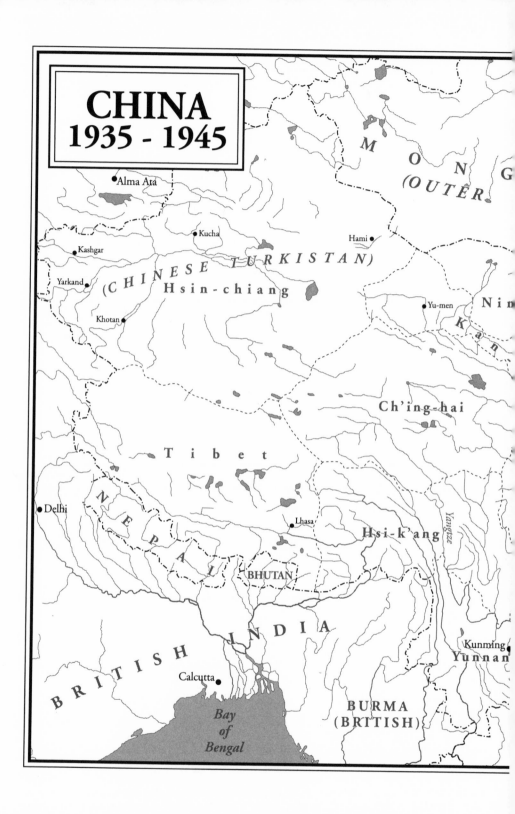

CHINA
1935 - 1945

Alma Ata

M O N G
(OUTER

Kucha

Hami

Kashgar

(C H I N E S E   T U R K I S T A N)

Yarkand

Hsin-chiang

Yu-men

N i n

Khotan

K a n

Ch'ing-hai

T i b e t

Delhi

N E P A L

Lhasa

Hsi-k'ang

BHUTAN

Yangtze

B R I T I S H   I N D I A

Kunming

Yunnan

Calcutta

Bay
of
Bengal

BURMA
(BRITISH)

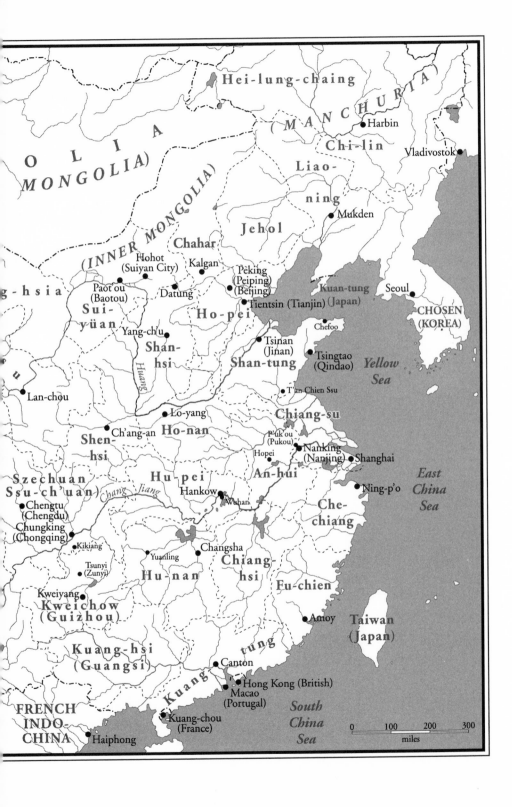

Chapter I

I sat in the gazebo in Eldest Brother-in-law's garden outside Nanking, practicing Chinese characters. The garden, which had evidently been well cared-for, was getting unkempt. The marigold plants were covered with dead blossoms. The chrysanthemums were budding but had not been pruned to produce big blooms.

The whole place had a deserted air.

The gardener had fled weeks before, along with the other servants, when my sister-in-law, Phoebe, took the children to Kuling. My brothers-in-law, Frank and Bill (they were all the kind of Chinese who like to use their English names), my husband, Wally, and a few friends were spending nights at the house to avoid the frequent night bombings of Nanking. When I came, seizing a rare opportunity to escape Japanese-held Tientsin, most people said that a woman should not stay. Only Wally said that, since I had no children, I could stay with him.

The house was a tiny, Western-style bungalow, tucked between the mansions of President Lin Sen, the ceremonial figurehead of the government, and Wang Ching-wei, who later became the puppet governor under the Japanese. Not far away we could see the Sun Yat-sen mausoleum and the Purple Mountain, over which the Japanese planes flew to bomb the city.

It was the fall of 1937. Since the war with Japan began at Lu K'ou Chiao (Marco Polo Bridge) in July, the news had always been bad. The Japanese were rapidly taking over North China and the seacoast. Shanghai, desperately defended, could not hold out much longer. Wally had come to Nanking to take a new job before the war began, leaving me to finish my school year in Tientsin. I was caught by the war and could not get away until late August. Now I was enjoying an idyllic life, recovering from the tension of the summer. A distant cousin, glad to escape the city, had come to run the household. I had little to do except study Chinese, iron the men's washable khaki suits, and try to make by hand some of the clothes we would need for winter.

I had time to think how I had got into such a situation. Why had I come to China?

Coming back from a year of study in Europe in 1933, I had found America in the depths of the depression. After a year of unemployment I triumphed over one hundred other applicants to get a teaching job which proved intolerable. The crisis came at a staff meeting which dragged on for hours. We would not be allowed to leave until we each *volunteered* to sponsor an after-school club of some kind.

A friend and I supported each other in stubborn resistance.

We already had eight classes a day, with no prep time, and our salaries had been cut from $125 a month to $107.78. It was late. We were tired and hungry. One teacher after another initialled something on the list and left the room. With a gesture of defeat, I signed for camera club and she for botany, and we headed for the door.

"That settles it," I said, "I'm going to China."

She said, "I wish I had a China to go to, or any place at all. My folks would think I was insane if I gave up a job in these times."

My sister in Tientsin had told me she could get me a job teaching English. My father lent me the steamer fare. So here I was, married to a Chinese economist, sitting in a gazebo, waiting for the sound of bombing planes to send me to the dugout in the garden.

Thinking back to the beginning, I have confused memories of long, gray days on the Pacific, five sparkling days in Tokyo and Nikko, and a little ship on which I was the only non-Japanese, tossing in the tail of a typhoon.

With the approach to the China coast my memories become as clear as etchings. I can picture as if I had seen them yesterday the first surge of yellow water around the ship at sea, the broad, yellow sweep of river, limited on either side by yellow clay and yellow, mud-walled villages, children playing by the water's edge, and the magical emerald green of the fields and trees. I stood on deck the whole morning, taking in every detail of the passing scene, and at noon we came to Tangku, the port for Tientsin.

My sister Emily had brought a man from the China Travel Service to help me. He whisked me through Customs, and we got on the next train for Tientsin. Emily was delighted to see that Chinese already looked like individuals to me. Newcomers often think they all look alike, as we also do to them. Her first concern was to teach me the Chinese character for *woman* so I could know which door to go through in case of need.

"We'll walk home," said Emily as we left the train. "It's very near."

We traversed an open, dusty place, a short distance of wide motor road, and a narrow, rutted, unpaved street.

"We'd like to find another house," she said. "This one's too near the station in case of bombing."

That was my introduction to living under the shadow of war.

The house was a hybrid of a kind common in Tientsin. The layout around a courtyard was essentially Chinese, but there were glazed casement windows and metal door fixtures instead of the traditional decorative lattices and wooden hinges and bolts. The more important rooms had wooden floors instead of tamped earth. It had been a snug fit for Emily's family: her husband, Shou-yu, two-year-old Ben, her aged father-in-law, a student nephew, a woman servant and a puppy. For me the only resource was a bed in the living room.

Housekeeping arrangements seemed primitive to me. The kitchen was dark, with only the few pieces of equipment needed to make delicious Chinese food. Clothes were scrubbed on wooden washboards and ironed with troublesome irons that had to be heated in the firehole of the stove. There were no sanitary facilities in our sense of the word. Emily had caused a cesspool to be built so the kitchen slops didn't have to be carried out in buckets. Floors were mopped daily. Rubbish was not allowed to accumulate in the yard. Otherwise we lived like our neighbors.

But my introduction to such a life was to be postponed. Shou-yu was away on a business trip, and Emily had planned a holiday to let me glimpse the real China before settling down to a school year in Tientsin, a city she disliked.

After only one night in the little house, we caught the express train for Peking, which in those days was called Peiping, left little Ben with a friend at Yenching University, and went jogging in rickshaws to the Western Hills, the mountains that rise out of the plain a few miles from the city. Barred by rumors of bandits from the fairyland of T'an Chieh Ssu, we chose the safe and sane YMCA hostel at Sleeping Buddha Temple. There we passed long, lazy, beautiful days, walking to scenic spots in the mornings, sleeping through the dripping heat of the day, and going at sunset to play among the hot rocks in a mountain stream, where we washed our clothes.

In those few days I learned to love China, and the friendly, old-fashioned country people who marveled that I came from "outside the sea."

At the end of a week our money was stolen by a sneak thief so nervous that he left behind the instrument with which he pried open my locked suitcase. The manager cancelled our bill. With our pocket money we took rickshaws back to Yenching, where we stayed for another two weeks, going often into Peiping to sightsee and to visit friends.

One day there was a gathering of former Carleton College students to celebrate my arrival. Carleton College is a small liberal arts college located in Northfield, Minnesota, the town I grew up in. Among them was Wally Liu, who had been my classmate. After lunch Emily, Wally and I sat under an ancient cedar tree at the Temple of Heaven and drank tea and ate melon seeds all through the long, hot afternoon.

I thought, "I had forgotten how nice he is."

Later I found that he had thought the same about me.

Back in Tientsin I awaited the opening of school, preparing my courses and accustoming myself to the heat, which lay like a thick mulch over the city. Shou-yu returned and began house-hunting, not an easy task for a family that wanted wooden floors.

School began. I was teaching at the Women's Normal College of Hopei, one of the few places in China where a girl could get a really modern education. Sixteen hours a week of English and French seemed like gilded luxury after the day-long grind of the high school. I added to my schedule a weekly conference with each student, and still I felt leisured. Only later did I learn that the normal teaching load was twelve hours a week.

I soon found out that a teacher in China was not an underpaid oddity, as at home, but enjoyed a privileged position suitable to the esteem in which scholarship has always been held in that country. There were some things in that revolutionary generation that had no place in school discipline as I conceived it. The students' right to strike, and to demand the dismissal of an ineffective teacher, seemed anarchistic to me, though I had known teachers who deserved such treatment.

After a month we found a house—far larger than we needed—for only twenty-five Chinese dollars a month. It was old and shaky, but the main parts had wooden floors, and the rooms were arranged around a really spacious paved yard. Before moving in we sealed doors and windows and boiled formalin to destroy vermin, and had three cartloads of rubbish removed from the yard. A cesspool was dug in a small service courtyard by the kitchen.

When spring came we lifted paving stones to plant trees and make flower beds. Vines of gourd and morning glory and vegetable sponge softened the gray brick walls and the wooden spirit screen inside the gate. Bamboo long chairs tempted one to linger in the yard. A structure of poles lashed together and covered with mats provided shade, without which outdoor living in summer would have been impossible. This was the *liang p'ung*, a legacy of the Mongols, expert tent makers, who ruled China in the thirteenth century.

My room, on a small side court, which was my home for a year and a half, was long and airy, with a leaky skylight. I had yellow curtains, lampshades and cushions, yellow pottery tea things, red lacquer boxes and a bamboo long chair. For my share of the rent, meals, laundry and all services I paid Emily thirty-five Chinese dollars a month, or about fourteen American dollars at the prevailing exchange rate.*

Except for the sense of spaciousness, the housekeeping arrangements were about the same as in the old house, electricity being the only modern convenience. I often fumed at the apparently unnecessary inefficiency, and hinted to Emily that if I were in her place I'd do something about it. She smiled tolerantly and said she didn't think I would. I hadn't been in China long enough to understand the futility of fretting over non-essentials, or to know what *was* non-essential. Besides, she pointed out, although she had no modern conveniences, she had the old-fashioned convenience of a servant to bear the brunt of the inconvenience.

A disagreeable feature of our life was the rudeness of the children in the street, who ran after us shouting, "Foreign hairy creature smokes opium!" They called us hairy because Chinese have very little body hair. The connection with opium came from the fact that the British fought two wars to force China to import opium (previously forbidden) from India to restore the British trade balance.

I have never met such rudeness outside Tientsin, though I suppose it would be found in any treaty port having a large and exclusive foreign

*NOTE: It was usual to refer to the Chinese unit of currency as a dollar when speaking English because it was based on the Mexican silver dollar, although in 1935 the exchange rate with U. S. dollars was about three to one. In Chinese it was called a *k'uai*, and was worth about as much in China as an American dollar was in America. References to dollars in this book are all Chinese unless otherwise stated.

element. Wherever I have gone in the interior I have heard people say, "Oh, a foreigner!" and sometimes discuss my big feet or my strange appearance, but it was only interest, not hostility. Chinese have told me that in America they are tormented by white children chanting "Ching Chong Chinaman eats dead rats!" in cities that have a Chinatown, but not elsewhere. It seems that any exclusive group sets itself up to be treated as outsiders by those whom it excludes.

At that time only a handful of foreigners lived in the Chinese sections of Tientsin. The large European communities and most of the higher class Chinese were crowded into the British, French, Italian and Japanese concessions, areas where by treaty they were not subject to Chinese law, but only to their own courts. They enjoyed modern houses, wide streets, luxurious marketing facilities, and a kind of security in case of war. Every time the threat of war flared up, more of the Chinese with means moved into the concessions. The Chinese city, thus drained of the element that could have kept it in order, was dirty, disorderly and down-at-heel beyond anything I have since seen in interior cities, even in war time.

The Americans had no concession because after the Boxer uprising in 1900, they did not join the other powers in demanding punitive damages, but instead used their share of the reparations money to build Tsinghua University in Peiping.

In spite of the dinginess, we preferred to live in the Hopei (North of the River) district. Shou-yu wanted to be near his factory, I liked being within walking distance of my school, and Emily detested the spurious Europeanism of the concessions. Whenever the atmosphere grew tense we stocked up on flour and rice and staples such as cabbage, onions and eggs, and sat tight.

I made good friends among the foreign community, but like Emily I could bear to breathe the air of the concessions only a few times a month, Such visits left us with a sense of disproportion and unreality. A few examples may show what I mean.

I met a woman who had been a friend of my predecessor. She said she was sorry for me. I didn't see why. The school was pleasant, my colleagues cooperative, and the pay good.

"Huh! You wouldn't find two hundred a month much if you lived down here. You really ought to come down and live with us, though. You'd be so much happier. There's an empty room in the house where our crowd stay."

She invited me to have tea with her the following Saturday.

I found a large, gloomy house, elaborately furnished in Western style with oriental refinements such as Peking rugs and carved blackwood tea tables. Everyone else had gone out, so we two sat down to a tea prepared for a dozen people. We were faultlessly served by English-speaking servants. I said that the foreign cakes and sandwiches tasted good for a change.

"Do you mean to say you don't have them every day?"

"No. We eat Chinese food."

"Ugh! How can you stand it? Isn't it horribly greasy, frying everything as they do?"

"No, I like it."

"Well, I'm sure I could never stand it."

"How long have you been in China?"

"I was born here."

Born in China, she had learned nothing of the country except how to live as nearly as possible as if she were somewhere else.

Tea over, she put her arm around me and led me up the stairs to her own room.

"How about it? Don't you think you'd better come down here to live? You'll die of boredom out there, and it's so filthy everywhere, and the Chinese food will ruin your health."

I again professed my satisfaction with my living arrangements, and she invited me to have a game of Tiddly-winks.

I didn't know then that Tiddly-winks was an intercollegiate sport in England. I thought of it as a childhood pastime. I pretended to be interested in the antics of the chips.

"I have several games here. I had them sent out from Home. Life is so dull, and we need something to do after school hours. I'll give you a game to take home with you. You can play with Emily. You'll find it helps."

Refusing with thanks, I fled. I did not begrudge her the pitiful luxury of feeling sorry for me.

A friendship I valued was that of a French army family. I well remember the perfect French dinners, complete with imported wine, Captain Vastel's shrewd comments on life and the world, Madame's discursive narratives, and the quiet "*Oui, Maman*" of Mademoiselle Louise, who was looking forward to a prudent transaction on the marriage market when they returned to France.

Madame was worried that, living and working where I did, I might follow Emily's example and marry a Chinese. She schemed to bring me into contact with eligible bachelors. One of her bright hopes for me centered on an Italian gentleman, well past his first youth, who made a good living stuffing Latin and mathematics into Mlle. Louise and other young members of the French and Italian communities. At the dinner she arranged to bring us together, Mme. Vastel boasted artlessly about my ability to speak Chinese.

"Mademoiselle is young, and does not understand the dangers of her position," murmured the gentleman kindly. "Perhaps I may be pardoned a word of advice. During my twenty years' experience in China I have noticed that all those who study the language begin insensibly to take on the Chinese point of view."

"But why," I asked innocently, "would anyone wish to live for twenty years in China without understanding the Chinese point of view?"

Madame's generous hopes for us exploded, and the talk became the exercise in intellectual unreality so dear to their kind.

In the Chinese city most of the small transactions of everyday life were done in copper coins, whose value was about twenty-two for ten cents. We always went out with a small bag of coppers for rickshaw or tram fare, and the *amah* took coppers to market. At one time some maneuver that I still don't understand drained the coppers away and almost paralyzed business. When one made any small purchase one paid with a ten-cent note and got a scrap of paper with the shop's seal in place of change. This makeshift scrip passed freely in the neighborhood, to be redeemed eventually by the shop that issued it. Rickshaws and streetcars were the biggest problem, as they could neither accept nor issue scrip. One must pay ten cents for a three-copper run, or walk.

During this crisis Emily and I went to visit an English friend in the British Concession. Leaving, we remarked on the problem of paying tram fare without coppers.

"Oh, you need coppers? I have a big drawerful. The cook brings them home from market and I've never known any use for them."

We borrowed a valise and took home five dollars' worth.

Chapter 2

There was much that was sordid and ugly and depressing in this city with its dismal contrasts. I was too aware of the smug foreign concessions and the shabby Chinese city; the elegant homes of the foreign business men and retired warlords who skimmed the cream, and the thin kimonos of White Russian prostitutes who drank the dregs; the arrogance of the Japanese drug barons, and the abjectness of whining, heroin-addicted beggars; the white women shopping for Paris frocks and old porcelain, and the haggard women and children coming out of a Japanese cotton factory on the next street. Interesting it was, indeed, but not comfortable. There was nothing in it of the harmony of a real Chinese city. It was a vortex of ruthless, conflicting interests, all underscored by the constant pressure of Japanese encroachment.

Beggars in America and such parts of Europe as I have seen are few and comparatively well fed and well dressed. Nothing had prepared me to face the ragged hordes of them I now saw, with their practiced wails, their carefully show-cased physical defects, and their peculiar organization. Coming out from a feast in a fashionable restaurant, where dish after dish left the table half-eaten, I would have to push through a jungle of claw-like outstretched hands. Some knelt by the road, and when my rickshaw passed by they banged their heads on the ground, wailing, "O Great Aunt, give me one! Do a good deed!" The hardest to resist were the children, who were used by Fagin-like big beggars. To give to them would only cause more children to be used that way.

Although I knew that giving to beggars encouraged the racket, I also knew that there were many people down on their luck and desperate. Begging was regarded as a legitimate resource in time of trouble. Thus the problem was to strike a balance between being insensitive and being a sucker.

Many of the beggars showed the gray skin and dull eyes of drug addicts. Opium, identified in Western minds with China, has always been forced on China from outside, first by the British in the two Opium Wars, and now by the Japanese. Opium, however, was benign compared to the heroin which now flooded the country. The drug trade seemed to have become an instrument of Japanese policy in the campaign to gain possession of North China. Under extraterritoriality the Japanese Concession provided a safe haven, and the Korean nationals who carried on the trade outside the concession, being Japanese subjects, were immune to prosecution under Chinese law.

I served on a committee of the American Association of University Women to study the drug situation in Tientsin. Our report was so dark and terrifying that it was never allowed to be published. One detail that I remember is that in one block of the Japanese Concession there were more than ninety little booths where poor people lined up for their daily injection of heroin at a few coppers each. For people with money there was no lack of more comfortable facilities.

Every cold winter night dozens or even hundreds of bodies were found in the streets. Most of them were near the Japanese Concession, heading away from it, and with the marks of drug addiction. These were the ones who couldn't make it home after their injection. The Japanese had their own ways of disposing of those who fell within their jurisdiction, so the Chinese police reported only those who got across the border before they fell. No device was spared to make new addicts. Narcotized candy, cigarettes and patent medicines trapped the unwary, their Japanese brands saving them from prosecution. Most noteworthy were the red pills sold everywhere as a cure for the opium habit. They contained heroin, thus substituting a deadly habit for a merely degenerative one.

Aside from the demoralization of the Chinese people and the enormous financial profit, the Japanese gained another advantage from their narcotics program. It gave them a horde of slaves, devoid of will power, ready to commit crimes, become spies, march in demonstrations, or do anything rather than be deprived of their daily dose. Japanese subjects were strictly forbidden to use drugs and would be severely punished for it.

It must be understood that North China was all but under Japanese control for years before the war broke out. Manchuria had been taken in 1931, and it was clear that it was only a matter of time before North China also would be seized. The Central Government, playing for time to exterminate the Communists, accepted many preposterous demands, such as that for a demilitarized zone extending some distance south of Peiping. This was supposed to serve as a buffer, but in fact it was cleared only of Chinese troops. The Japanese maneuvered there at will.

While the Western world looked on with contempt at the sight of China swallowing insult after insult without fighting back, we in the northern provinces learned how slaves must feel, complying with ridiculous demands, and turning our eyes away from outrages that were beyond our power to help.

The students were the hardest element to control. They went on strike, paraded in the streets, harangued the illiterate, printed patriotic pamphlets, and sang the forbidden songs about the loss of Manchuria which later became the national war cries. They sent delegations to Nanking to demand action from the government, and all too often they did not return from such missions.

At last Chiang Kai-shek, who had taken to himself the title of Generalissimo, answered the insistent question, "When will China fight?"

"At the moment," he said, "when I would be forced to sign away any portion of China's territorial or adminstrative integrity."

That meant that Japan's gains could be ignored as long as they were not officially recognized, and so could be repudiated later without breach of faith. How Chiang thought he could reverse a *fait accompli* we didn't know.

Just before Christmas, 1935, it became known that the government was about to accede to a Japanese demand to set up an East Hopei Autonomous Region, a fancy name for a Japanese puppet state including Peiping. The students of all the colleges and universities in Peiping and Tientsin, many thousands, took to the streets in a massive demonstration, my students among them. They were dispersed by force, and kept under guard in their schools for some time, but they did succeed in forcing the government to delay the establishment of the Autonomous Region.

For months we in Tientsin watched the construction of a fortress at the entrance to the Japanese Concession. It was called a sub-police station. A formidable pile of reinforced concrete masked with brick, it dominated the approach on Asahi Road, the Japanese section of the main thoroughfare. Nothing, we said, would happen until it was finished.

Although the prospect of war was always in the back of our minds, it occupied only a small place in our thoughts. We went on making plans for the future just as if the future were a thing one could plan.

It seemed to me, too, that most Chinese had no concept of what war on a national scale would be. They had seen so many petty, local conflicts that they felt like veterans. If there should be a war, one would simply move out of the way for a while until things settled down.

I had seen the reconstructed battlefields of Europe, and known the generation of young people who had been children in the first World War. I sometimes tried to explain to people how different a national war would be from the little warlord tussles they had known, but I made no impression. I, after all, had never seen a war, and they had.

Chapter 3

Summer died and winter came. Tientsin has no autumn, as we northern Americans understand the word, no glory of red and purple and gold under a brilliant sky. The world just dries up, and the sun becomes faint, and snow comes. Then the windows are sealed all around with strips of paper, and if the family is modern, little coal stoves are set up in every room.

I put on my warmest winter sports clothes and thick, woolen ski socks, and always sat as near the stove as I could. My students held rubber hot water bottles under their coats in the classroom and warmed their hands on them when they were not writing. As they were forbidden to wear anything over their blue cotton gowns in school, a servant would warn them when an inspector was coming. Then they would quickly take off their coats and sit on them. Only in my steam-heated office, or in bed with a hot water bottle, was I ever warm that first winter.

Emily and Shou-yu wore Western clothes and shivered like me, but the rest of the household dressed for winter in traditional style, with padded gowns that came high around the neck, padded trousers and thickly padded shoes. They could not get used to keeping doors shut, although we constantly shouted at them about it. They moved in and out of the house and across the courtyard with apparent indifference to the cold, showing discomfort only when they came too close to our blazing stove.

Shou-yu's old father came to meals with us. Afterward he liked to sit in the living room a while to be sociable, but while we three sat hugging the fire he sat in the farthest corner. Soon the heat was too much for him and he withdrew to his own room, which was heated by the only old-fashioned brick bed in the house.

At that time I thought the *k'ang*, or brick bed, a clumsy and primitive device, but I now realize that it is the best way of heating a North China house in a North China winter. A small fire, lighted for a short time, circulates hot air through a system of flues in a brick platform, which becomes comfortably warm to sit or lie on. The bricks retain the heat for hours, radiating it gently to take the chill from the whole room. In some cases the fire can be built from outside, so that no smoke or ash sullies the room itself. In other cases the cooking fire does the job. The combination of warm clothing and an evenly panel-heated room is far more healthful than our way of great fires and poorly-designed clothes.

My second year I had a Chinese gown made of soft, brown silk, lined with green, and padded with a whole pound of camel hair. Under it I wore knitted pants that came just to the knee so they wouldn't show through the side slits, and a thin sweater. It was light and soft, quick to put on and easy to wear, and it gave me a sublime indifference to stoves. I could move around the house or classroom as I pleased. Emily and Shou-yu soon followed my example, and we graduated to a new level of winter living. We never put on Western clothes except for visits to the concessions.

The first time I wore the new gown to school I was amazed at the reaction. I had supposed that Chinese dress was traditional so that I would be correct in imitating what I had seen on others. I was not prepared to have the students gather around me and whoop, "That's last year's fashion!" I had a contrasting lining and two rows of satin binding, while the current style demanded a matching lining and one row of binding.

For all of my first semester I kept my nose happily to the grindstone. I enjoyed the personal contacts with the students, although I had a problem in trying to liven up the classroom. If I tossed a question to the class as a whole there would be no response. It had to be addressed to an individual, and so expressed as to spare her any possible embarrassment. The same women who were full of questions and ideas in their conversation or compositions would never risk losing face by asking a question in the group, expressing an original viewpoint, or admitting that they did not understand what I said. As a result I found the classes dull. I had to do most of the talking, and I could never be sure I was understood. They would listen just as attentively and nod just as politely when they had no idea what I was saying. I kept on talking anyway, as only by much listening would they ever learn to follow spoken English.

One day I went home at noon and found Wally there. I was surprised at my pleasure in seeing him. When I returned from my afternoon conferences, he had gone out. Knowing he would be there for supper and the night, I lay down for a nap. As often happened, I fell into such deep sleep that when the *amah* came to call me to supper I only murmured, "I don't want any," and dozed off again until morning. Wally has never let me forget this display of indifference.

When winter vacation came I enjoyed it as one can do only after a long stretch of unbroken routine. Emily arranged for me to stay with friends at the American Board Mission in Peiping. I wrote to Wally to meet me, as I was still afraid of the rush of porters and rickshaw men at the station. He promptly adopted me, filling my days with the sightseeing and excursions that are so easy in and around Peiping.

We explored the Hall of Ancestors, the Lama Temple, the Forbidden City, the parks, and the Jade Fountain. We spent all of one glorious, sunny day rambling around the Summer Palace and the Tibetan style ruins behind it. We warmed our cold feet at a variety of eating places, enjoying Mongolian style mutton cooked in a charcoal kettle on the table; crisp curls of fat duck, roasted on a spit and wrapped in thin, unleavened pancakes with green onions and a savory sauce; fried duck livers; spare ribs with sugar and vinegar, and countless other creations which, once tasted, leave nostalgic memories forever.

My vacation passed quickly. Back at work I could no longer keep my whole attention on lectures and compositions. Spring was in the air, and Tientsin stifled me. I had my work arranged so that I could catch the express for Peiping on Saturday morning and return Sunday evening. My kind friends at the mission were ideal hostesses, showing no surprise when I dropped my bag in their house at lunch time and dashed off without eating, or showed up just in time to tumble into bed. I usually had Sunday breakfast with them, and then disappeared until train time.

The weather grew milder. Who could resist the long donkey rides into the hills to temples and parks that have made the people of Peiping holiday-minded for a thousand years? Sometimes it was a mad scramble to catch a bus back to town. Missing the express, I might have to take a local train that wheezed along for three or four hours. There might be no time for dinner, and Wally would run to buy chocolate bars, thrusting them into my hands as the train started.

After such a weekend I could again work with enthusiasm, but by Saturday I was tired of talking and talking. It was a relief to settle down in the train and not talk, and then to be with Wally, to whom I didn't have to say anything unless I had something to say.

I had learned in Europe that the place to get to know the people of a country is in the third-class railroad cars. That is where you see the local people in the course of their everyday business. In China, also, I loved to travel third class.

Seats of bare wood faced each other in pairs, and between them, by the window, was a little shelf with teapot and cups. For a few coppers an attendant would keep replenishing the pot, with a flourish of a long-spouted tea kettle which somehow never did scald the passengers. People who had rigid inhibitions against eating on the street had none at all about stuffing themselves on the train. They hung roast chickens, varnished with a shiny, red sauce, from hooks above the tea shelf until they felt like tearing them apart and devouring them. They took long, thin cucumbers from their pockets and ate them skin and all. They tossed orange peels and peanut shells and melon seed skins on the floor, from where they were swept up occasionally. They split large turnips into wedges and consumed them raw. At every stop they opened the windows and bought little, round sesame seed cakes,and long strips of fried batter, or bowls of noodles, or soybean milk with poached egg, or fragrant almond soup. They bought local specialties of any kind for gifts to friends at journey's end.

Mothers unbuttoned their clothes and nursed their babies, and then held them out over a cuspidor while making an efficacious hissing sound. If it was warm, men took off their long gowns and sat in the soft pajama suits which are both underwear and lounging apparel. Everybody fanned when it was hot. Some looked at nobody, others prattled cheerfully to the car at large about their affairs. Any occidental who looked at all receptive would probably find someone eager to practice his English.

Luggage seemed to be limited only by the problem of getting it aboard. Besides valises and suitcases there were oilskin bedding rolls, bundles tied up in squares of cloth, baskets of all sizes, some filled with chickens or fruit going to market, and practically any size or shape of object that could pass through the door.

In this connection, I could observe the workings of Japanese commerce. A steady stream of Japanese goods was smuggled into Tientsin from the north, by the South Manchurian Railway. Not content with having evaded Customs duty, its owners wanted to avoid paying for its transportation to the interior. Gangs of Koreans (Japanese subjects at that time) waited on the station platform, laden with bales of cotton cloth and manufactured goods of every description. When a train pulled in, one member of each gang jumped aboard a third-class car and opened a window. The others quickly passed him bales, bundles and boxes, which he piled on the seats and racks and even in the aisle around him. By the time other passengers could get aboard they often found no place to sit, unless on their own luggage in the aisle.

If the police or the armed guards that rode on every train tried to interfere, they came up against extraterritoriality. To arrest a Japanese subject was to risk an international incident. Even if one were arrested, he must be turned over to the Japanese court, which would say he had broken no Japanese law.

∾

Wally and I have never been able to decide just when we began to consider ourselves engaged. There was never a formal proposal or acceptance, but lots of serious discussion.

"If we should get married," he said, "it's not at all certain that you could ever go home again."

"Women since time began have married into distant countries."

"Life may be terribly hard. You know we're due for a big war one of these days."

"You have to face it, so why shouldn't I? But what will your parents say if you marry a foreign devil?"

"They may need a while to get used to it, but they will like you and then it will be all right. How about your parents?"

"When I was in Europe my aunt wrote to me that I mustn't marry anyone far from home because my mother needed a daughter nearby. When Mother found out about it she called my aunt a meddlesome old woman, and told me it was nobody's business but mine whom I married."

So, little by little, we reached a definite decision. I remember a day when, sitting in the exquisite national library in Peiping, and looking through the window at the graceful ceramic tile gateway that gleamed against a deep blue sky, I felt a flood of happiness at the thought that this brave, beautiful country was now my home.

Willing and eager though I was to make all necessary adjustments to life in China, there were some that I thought ought not to be made. As an American, my impulse was to adapt my environment to me, rather than me to it. It was all very well, I argued, to spend my life in China, but that didn't have to mean keeping house the way Emily did. I should have the gumption to set a material standard below which I would not fall.

I did some serious thinking about what things were necessary for domestic comfort and convenience. I did not wish to match an American home, but only to show, as I thought, what could be done by any family of moderate means.

I sent an order to Montgomery Ward's export department for a treadle sewing machine, a clothes wringer, a cyclone washer, a steam pressure cooker, and a few lesser things. Had it not been for later developments beyond my control, I would probably have carried out my idea of trying to teach others how to live, instead of learning from them, and the next nine years would have been more comfortable, but far less interesting.

For all our brave reasoning, we waited apprehensively for the first reactions of our families to our plans. We might as well have relaxed. Wally's mother had been so discouraged because four of her five sons seemed to scorn matrimony that she was ready to welcome almost any match. The reactions of my family were summed up by my older brother, who had spent three years in Peiping. He quoted a Chinese proverb to the effect that a bad egg at home cannot compare with a good egg abroad.

Chapter 4

Wally found a job in a military academy in Kwangsi, run by dissident generals Li Tsung-jen and Pai Chung-hsi. Before he could start work the school was closed by order of Chiang Kai-shek. Wally came back to Tientsin with six months' severance pay in his pocket, and we proceeded with our plans. We signed papers at the municipal government for the Chinese side, and got a representative from the American consulate to witness a simple ceremony performed by Bob Chandler of the American Board Mission.

We set up housekeeping in a rented room in the British Concession with a Russian landlord and his meddlesome Rumanian mistress. The Chinese cook helped us with our cooking, and a Japanese dance hall girl in the other room entertained us with her misadventures.

Late in April we left on a trip to Pailingmiao, the temple far out in the Mongolian desert which had been the Japanese headquarters during their failed coup the preceding fall, by which they had intended to sever Mongolia from China. We went with a tour group of students and teachers from my college and Peiping University. We had three third-class sleeping cars and a diner, which were side-tracked wherever we wanted to sightsee, and then hitched to the next day's train. This was a marvelous, uncomplicated way to travel.

We had twenty-four hours in Kalgan, where we visited the marketplace and marveled at the cascades of silver jewelry on Mongolian princesses whose clothes and hair had never been washed. Then we stopped for a day at Datung, where we took buses to a mountainside covered with hundreds of Buddhist cave sculptures.

I didn't know that since the fighting, foreigners weren't allowed in that area. It was impossible to exclude Japanese except by excluding all foreigners. Somewhere before we got to Suiyuan City our cars were sidetracked beside the private car of the governor, Fu Tso-yi. He saw Wally and me walking along the track and sent someone to investigate the illegal foreigner. Learning that I was a teacher on the way to Pailingmiao with my students, he sent orders ahead for no one to interfere with me.

In Suiyuan the governor invited our group to dinner. Thinking this was just part of the tour package, I said I wanted to find a horse to ride instead. What was the use of coming to Mongolia if I couldn't ride one of the Mongolian ponies? Wally and I were out looking for a horse when Fu Tso-yi's secretary came in a car to find us because the dinner was in my honor! So Wally and I, in riding clothes, sat on either side of General Fu Tso-yi while he told us how he had routed the Japanese from Pailingmiao.

Years earlier, he said, the Japanese had sent young army officers to become monks at the temple. They had fortified it, and worked to win the Mongol princes away from their loyalty to China. When it seemed that the time was right, the army came and launched the attack which was supposed to "free" Mongolia from China.

The fighting was bitter through the fall, but Fu Tso-yi, choosing his time, sent men by truck to within thirty miles of the temple. Picked units went ahead on foot through snow and cold, and stormed the temple gate at five in the morning. The rest came up by truck, arriving soon after them. They subdued the temple and destroyed the Japanese command. With their headquarters gone, the soldiers out fighting in the desert were soon mopped up.

The ride up to Pailingmiao, by army truck, was wild. It took ten hours to go one hundred twenty miles. The first part was up a dry river bed where a road had been made by throwing the larger rocks aside. In some places the so-called road had become so rutted that the drivers preferred to drive over among the rocks. We stopped from time to time for distribution of Dramamine to those who needed it.

Once up the mountains onto the desert plateau, the driving was easy as long as the air was clear. We had a clean wind until a few minutes before we got there. We stood up in the open trucks, holding onto the iron bars above our heads, and sang to the wide horizon. Then a dust storm struck, cutting visiblity and scouring our skin.

We spent a night at the temple, and were shown the elaborate defenses that the Japanese monks had built, and the big Buddhas whose stomachs had been emptied of their treasures when the real monks fled to the hills. Instead of the gold and jewels which a Buddha often holds, these turned out to have only hundreds of tiny clay Buddhas with fine details. I was given one of them for a souvenir.

The colonel in charge let me ride his own horse, a tough-looking buckskin pony with the gaits of an angel. It galloped up and down the

Bea and Wally (Liu Hsing-hwa) on their wedding day, at Emily's house, February 8, 1937. Bea is wearing her "out-of-date" padded gown.

parade ground and then out onto the desert and back. It was heavenly.
I had felt that a trip to Mongolia would be wasted if I didn't get a
chance to ride one of those ponies.

The soldiers were kept busy reforesting the hills and building
roads. They set out thousands of such trees as could grow in that sandy
soil, and carried water in Standard Oil tins to water them. All the army
trucks were Ford V-8's.

From Suiyuan City we went to Paot'ou, the end of the railroad,
and saw the area that was being irrigated with water from the Yellow
River. Large numbers of settlers were coming on every train, with their
wordly goods in big, net-covered baskets. The government was subsidiz-
ing them to go up there and start farming. The leaders of the project
were an ex-general and his wife, who had got fed up with the corruption of political life. They were living like the people and promoting improved agricultural methods.

From Paot'ou it was a twenty-four hour run back to Peiping, and
then the usual two hours to Tientsin and my final term at the college.

During all this, Emily had calmly produced a baby named Sylvia. One
day I went to her house to do some accumulated laundry, and stayed
until evening, and then I hurried home. I found Wally, in lonely state,
picking at a roast chicken. He eyed me mournfully and said, "I was really
worried about your coming. I have to go to Nanking tomorrow."

Wally had a telegram from Elder Brother Frank asking him to go
to Nanking to apply for a job. I still had a month to go on my school
year. For some reason (to get the turbulent students safely home?) the
graduation date was moved up two weeks, so it was a hectic rush. When
it was over I moved back to Emily's house where I had more room to
work at packing for the move to Nanking.

On July 7 an apparently insignificant incident where the Japanese
were conducting maneuvers at Lu K'ou Ch'iao near Peiping gave
them an excuse to clash with the local forces. Fighting continued, but
no one was ready to call it war. The 29th Army, stationed in North
China, did what it could, but for a long time there was no support
from the Nanking government. Chiang Kai-shek was still determined
to kill all the Communists before facing the Japanese. As he was unwilling to commit his modern equipment, the 29th Army made much
use of big swords, produced on an emergency basis by all the black-

Bea on the colonel's horse, Pailingmiao, 1937. The pony was a tough,
responsive little buckskin.

smith shops in the area. China was ridiculed in the world press for opposing a modern army with swords.

Japanese planes often flew over and dropped slips of paper promising to protect the Chinese people from the Chinese army. We were so used to tension that it seemed natural.

One journal entry survives from that period.

Journal, Tientsin, July 14, 1937 (one week after Lu K'ou Ch'iao)

Morning paper—Generals Yen Hsishan and Fu Tsoyi are said to be ready to move in . . . Jingoism is said to be rife in Japan . . . Eight more Japanese troop trains have come from beyond Shanhaikwan . . . Barracks for Japanese civilians are being built in Peiping.

Afternoon—Po Wei reported five truckloads of dead Japanese on Huang Wei Lu, covered with white cloth but not effectively hidden, and a truck with five or six soldiers with ashy faces, staring vaguely about, evidently shell-shocked . . . also that Japanese troops tried to march out Huang Wei Lu to the motor road at three in the morning but were stopped by the 29th Army, so they marched around the new station and made a loop back to the road outside the city.

Evening news broadcast—Twenty nurses, five ambulances and a large quantity of medical supplies arrived in Tientsin . . . Nanking papers are openly demanding a showdown . . . Japanese have been assigned to the Peining railroad administration to direct traffic; they have already been making nuisances of themselves for days interfering with business . . . Korean troops are ready to move in . . . five hundred Korean coolies have been pressed into service.

I was helping Hsu-fen with her English lesson when Kwang-shiu came in goggle-eyed. He had been on Ta Ching Lu and was frightened by the Japanese he saw there. I asked what they were doing, but he couldn't say. I finished the lesson, took my evening sponge, and went out for a look around. I thought the neighbors were standing around in larger numbers than even such a hot evening would account for. When I reached Huang Wei Lu it was indeed full of Japanese, a row of loaded carts standing still as far as I could see each way, and the men sitting along the curb resting and smoking. I walked nearly to Ssu Ma Lu, where several soldiers crowded around a water jar, nearly blocking the sidewalk. I decided not to go any farther, but to call Po-wei and Hsu-fen to see. We all stood at the mouth of the hutung and watched as all kinds of military material passed on the way to the front: carts, men, Manchurian carts pulled by little Manchurian ponies, men on horseback, more carts, trucks full of men, men on bicycles, all going at a foot pace, trucks groaning in low gear.

Bea and Wally, summer, 1937.

A pause and then, from far up the street, a peculiar fluttering sound such as I had never heard. It must be infantry marching, but how different it sounds when it is really moving up to the front and not marching smartly on parade! First came coolies with shoulder poles and tools. Small wonder they didn't sound smart! Then came companies of trained infantry, but they still sounded funny. I watched the easy, relaxed gait, head forward, arms swinging. These men were really going into action, and the showy side of militarism had been shed like the Sunday suit it is, but they still didn't sound right. I watched them: slip-slog, slip-slog. Of course! How stupid of me! These were Japanese in leather shoes, and except for a few who have adapted successfully Japanese in leather shoes always sound funny. They set their toes down first with a forward sliding movement, as if they were walking in their own native clogs.

These men moving doggedly toward the front are conscripts, and although I know that many of them will come back piled in trucks, and that because of them truckloads of Chinese corpses will rumble toward wherever Chinese corpses are taken, and although the sights and sounds and even smells of a battlefield seem present in my senses as I look at them, and my heart swells with helpless wrath, the only emotion I can feel toward these slogging mortals is one of cosmic pity. They are as truly victims as China is.

I remember the nice, English-speaking taxi driver who squired me around Tokyo on my way to China. He wanted to marry a girl he was in love with, but he couldn't because he had been drawn for military service. He hated the whole idea. He would soon have been able to buy his own taxi and get married, but now he would have to go for two years and lose all his business. There was no escape for a poor man who was drawn. That was nearly two years ago. He should soon have been able to go back to his girl, but now conscripts whose terms expire are not to be released. I can almost hate the brains that have planned all this, but not the men, never the men.

Midnight—Emily and Shou-yu came in from a show. They saw marching troops on Asahi Road and estimated them at one thousand men. They saw another truckload of dead. There were three big sword battles today. The soldiers wore some kind of body armor to protect them from the swords, so all the corpses lacked a head, arm, or leg, these being the only parts the swords could reach. The whole world is laughing at China for fighting a modern army with swords, but it seems to be remarkably effective. Captain Vastel went out to observe, and he said the Chinese were fighting like lions. When will Chiang Kai-shek admit that the country is at war, and commit his modern equipment?

On July 27th I was ready to go. Shou-yu had sent a man from his sporting goods factory to put iron bands around my wooden boxes. I had a train reservation for the next day. A truck would come in the morning for my things.

That night the war came to us. From two a.m. on we could hear sporadic firing in several drections. By five there was a skirmish going on in our lane. We stayed on the far side of the house, away from the bullets.

In the morning the city was in Chinese hands. The 29th Army, knowing that there were few Japanese forces in the city just then, had fought its way down the motor road in the night. Now they seemed to be in control, and the people were in a mood of celebration.

But there were no trains running.

I spent the morning tearing into my baggage and choosing things to put into two suitcases and a knapsack that I could carry myself if there should be a way to go.

At two o'clock Shou-yu came to my room and told me to look at the sky. It was polka-dotted with Japanese bombers, each with two fighters. As we watched, they laid a pattern of bombs over the city.

We quickly organized the household. We put Ben and Sylvia (both sound asleep) under strong beds. We put Shou-yu's teen-age nephew and niece under the arch between living room and dining room, with pillows to put over themselves when planes came close. I sat opposite them in a stuffed chair, with more pillows, and entertained them with bad jokes in worse Chinese. The *amah* joined us. Shou-yu's father preferred to stay in his own room. Emily and Shou-yu circulated, keeping track of things, and diving under a table when planes came close.

After the first pattern bombing, the planes seemed to concentrate on specific targets. They worked all afternoon, shuttling back and forth from their air base only a few miles away. Our house shook and rattled many times, but stood. At five o'clock the bombing stopped.

A neighbor who had a telephone asked Emily to call the American consulate and ask to be evacuated. He thought if he followed close behind, he also might escape.

The consulate was emphatic. No one should try to go anywhere. We should make ourselves as safe as we could where we were. They would come for us when it was possible.

We lifted paving stones in the yard, dug a hole, set my heavy boxes of books around it, and covered it with the *pung* poles, an oilskin sheet, and the displaced earth. We were ready for what the morrow might bring.

I awakened with blisters on my hands, and remembered with satisfaction the shelter we had made. It seemed to define a new way of life, where we would meet external threats with personal action. The Japanese might dictate the circumstances, but our reaction to them was up to us.

We had breakfast with what there was in the house. I worked at refining my packing, choosing the few useful or precious things to go in my hand luggage. It was hopeless to get anything from the wooden boxes, which were now part of the shelter. I packed the most basic clothing for Wally and myself. He had gone to Nanking with only one suitcase of summer clothes. I must take him a good winter suit and a sweater, at least. I put in some non-essentials: my pocket-size copy of *The Prophet*, and a priceless little cloisonne vase that Wally used to hold writing brushes.

I wondered about my lack of feeling about abandoning the wooden boxes. When I packed them it had seemed urgent to get them to Nanking. Yesterday they were a welcome addition to the shelter. Today they only symbolized the new, simple goal of survival. With my essentials in a form I could carry myself, I was free to take any way that might open to get away to Wally.

After breakfast the neighbor came to say that the consulate was on the phone.

"Don't go anywhere," said a voice. "We're trying to come for you. Prepare minimum luggage to bring in the car."

It was raining hard. We busied ourselves with all kinds of little details. It occurred to us that it would be good to have an American flag to leave on the house. A Japanese would have only to sew a red circle on a white cloth, but to make the Stars and Stripes? The Stars and Stripes forever?

Emily tore one of Sylvia's diapers in half, dipped one half in red ink, and put it on the stove to dry. We cut forty-eight jagged bits of white and laid them in rows on a square of blue, putting one line of machine stitching through each row. Then the red was dry, and we began assembling the stripes. When we were still sewing on the twelfth stripe, John Stone, the vice-consul who had witnessed my wedding arrived. We nailed the incomplete flag to the door and went with him.

He had brought a Japanese vice-consul, Mr. Tanaka, to help him, and a family friend to show the way. The car had to hold them plus Emily and me, Ben and Sylvia, Shou-yu's father, a thirteen-year-old niece, and the *amah*. Obviously the luggage was limited. Shou-yu and his nephew stayed to take care of things.

Mr. Stone had news of what had happened. The most notable event was the total destruction of Nankai University, which had been a hot-bed of anti-Japanese activity. We had many friends at Nankai, and had often been to the beautiful campus.

We drove through heavy rain, by a roundabout route. Here and there we could see little sandbag redoubts and other evidence of the fighting, but all was quiet.

We came to the Japanese Concession by an unfamiliar street where the way was barred by an armor-plate gate. Mr. Tanaka got out and spoke through a little window. The gate glided silently back into the walls on either side, like something in a spy movie, and we went through, coming at last to Shou-yu's shop in the French Concession. There several employees vacated a small third-floor room for us, where we slept on trestle beds well supplied with bedbugs.

I had been troubled by a cough for several days. When we were ready to sleep I took a sip of cough medicine so as not to bother people with my barking. I was going to take another sip. When Emily got up at two to nurse Sylvia I woke up with the bottle still in my hand. I thought, "I must put this in a safe place." Then it was morning and the bottle was still in my hand.

Emily went to friends in the London Mission, who welcomed us to a house whose owner was away. Another couple was already there, Billy Baltau and his lovely Swedish wife from the Assemblies of God Mission in the Chinese city. When the fighting first began he called the consulate, and would not accept their advice to stay where he was. Loading his wife, his cook and lots of baggage onto rickshaws, he proceeded through the dark, dangerous streets to the concessions.

Sunday morning, after a good sleep in a comfortable bed, I wanted something to do. I went to the London Mission hospital next door and asked if they could use an extra pair of hands.

"Can you use a treadle machine?"

"I did as a child."

"Our sewing woman isn't here on Sunday, and no one knows how to use the machine. We have two hundred and fifty wounded coming in this afternoon and no draw sheets for them. Would you hem draw sheets?"

She took me to a room where a woman was tearing several bolts of unbleached muslin into suitable lengths. I inspected the ancient machine and soon had it whirring. The sheets were whisked away as fast as I could make them.

After a few hours I took a break to go and buy bug powder, which was important because we might have brought bugs with us to the mission house. As I left I met Mrs. Baltau and asked her if she would like to take my place at the machine for a while.

"Oh, I'd love to, but Billy wouldn't want me to do such a thing on Sunday."

That evening we went to see someone who had a radio, hoping for news. Most stations came in all right, but the one with the evening news from Nanking sounded like machine-gun fire. Our host said that earlier in the day he had heard Chiang Kai-shek announce that China had been pushed too far, and would fight. The Japanese evidently didn't want us to hear that.

People were going to the roof of a hotel to see what was going on in the Chinese city. We went, but could make no sense of the scattered fires and sounds of shooting. What was more interesting was the view through the windows of the top floor of the South Manchurian Railway building next door.

This building had long been suspected of being the center for Japanese espionage and smuggling activity. Now we saw a huge, brilliantly lighted room crammed with desks, at each of which sat a uniformed officer poring over maps or papers. Junior officers moved about, carrying papers from one to another, and here and there were two or three men in consultation.

"Their headquarters!"

That sight, plus the assurance that Chiang was going to fight, gave me a brief moment of physical dread. My mouth felt dry as I saw the military machine preparing to crush me.

If only it didn't keep me away from Wally!

Chapter 5

For the first few days after the bombing, rumors flew, but some of the facts were worse than the rumors. What hit us the hardest was the destruction of Nankai University. The American wife of a professor went to see what was left. Part of the library had survived, and soldiers were pouring gasoline on the books and burning them. She saw a valuable goldfish collection still intact, and tried to tell the soldiers that it was important. Their answer was to tip over the jars and pour the fish out on the ground.

As soon as things settled down a little, Shou-yu decided that he would be of more use if he joined us. He left his student nephew, Po-wei, in charge of the house, dressed himself in his pajama pants and a borrowed Chinese jacket, and set out to come to us. He telephoned from the Italian concession that he had got that far, losing his bicycle on the way, and was not allowed to enter the French or British concessions, which were already overwhelmed with refugees.

We consulted everyone we could think of. Madame Vastel offered to stand on the bridge and intercede for him when he came. Some missionaries were doing this for anyone who showed up with a Bible in his hands. What finally seemed best was simply to take a taxi and go and pick him up.

Thus we learned that a taxi with a White Russian driver was safe. Any car without a foreigner in it in the Chinese city would be commandeered by the Japanese. The Russian drivers, sons of refugees from the revolution, still looked like foreigners, though they were born in Tientsin and knew the city well. Emily and I would soon make big use of this information.

Po-wei called that the Japanese mopping-up party had stopped at the next house that day, and he expected them the first thing in the morning. He was scared. (Mopping up is a nice, neat name for the very messy process of cleaning out traces of resistance in conquered territory.)

What to do? Emily was nursing Sylvia and couldn't go. I didn't know the city except for the main streets, and my Chinese was sketchy. The choice was clear. I would go early in the morning, but I wanted a flag.

We went out and talked to rickshaw pullers, finding one who would be glad of a chance to check on relatives. He would wait for me at five in the morning.

Then we went looking for a flag. The only one we saw was one the size of a bed sheet on top of the Dollar Lines building. Emily remembered that Shou-yu's shop had red and white striped polo shirts. We banged on the door until a sleepy shop boy woke up and found us a shirt. Emily told me to get my sleep, and she would achieve a flag before morning. Like our earlier effort, it was crude but unmistakable.

The rickshaw man showed up promptly, took me to the house and waited for me. The twelve-stripe flag was still on the door, but our air raid shelter had vanished. Po-wei, hearing that other families had been shot for having such a thing, had dismantled it, cleaned the parts, refilled the hole, and taken plants from around the yard to make a flower bed where it had been.

Emily had told me to burn a scrap book she had kept over the years, documenting the Japanese encroachment. If it were found, it would be a death sentence for those in the house. I regret that I burned it. Had I been more experenced, I would have simply carried it downtown in my hand, but at that time I didn't know the extent of my privilege as an American.

I stayed with Po-wei most of the day, and the search party never came. Evidently the flag on the door did give protection. I took Po-wei back with me.

During the day I heard a paper boy shouting "*Yi Shih Pao.*" I knew that the highly-respected paper by that name, which had always been anti-Japanese, was not allowed to be taken out of the concessions. I sent Po-wei out to buy one and took it home with me. It was printed with the same paper, typeface and format as the genuine *Yi Shih Pao,* but the content was all pro-Japanese.

After that experience, Emily and I began to trust our wings. Mr. Tanaka, the Japanese vice-consul who had helped to rescue us, got us passes authorizing us to go and come as we pleased, but I seldom had to show mine. When we realized our power, we entered on a period of frenetic activity that I can scarcely believe as I look back on it. In fact, I couldn't believe it at the time. Where did we get the strength to go on and on, answering the incessant calls for help?

The Japanese wanted to be seen by the world as the heroic liberators of an oppressed people, so they were careful not to give a bad impression to foreigners. Chinese, on the other hand, were not safe outside the concessions. Emily and I were constantly on call to escort people who had important errands, or to do the errands for them. We were often offered fabulous sums for our services, but we refused. We didn't want to profit from misfortune. Our clients could pay for the taxi.

One exception was a merchant who wanted us to sit on a truck while he brought stock from his store. We agreed to make three trips to the store if he would make one to our house to bring our most important possessions. We found our makeshift flag still on the door, and the house unmolested. The roof had been badly damaged, and things were soggy.

One of my more interesting ventures was a visit to my old school, the Women's Normal College of Hopei. I had passed it several times, and seen that it had been bombed, but had not gone in. One day I met a man in a dirty Chinese gown, with a shaggy growth of beard. He identified himself as Mr. Chang, one of my fellow teachers, who had always been nattily dressed in foreign style. He had been out dancing in his tuxedo when the trouble started, and had not been able to get back to his room at the school. I told him I could take him there if he would meet me the next morning.

The gateman admitted us. In the whole college we found only scattered books and papers and half a piano. Mr. Chang's room had been sliced in half by a bomb. In the remaining half he found his book manuscript which had just been accepted for publication, his doctoral dissertation, and a few of his books. He was ecstatic. Then the gateman called that the Japanese were at the back gate, and we left in a hurry.

In my old office there was not so much as a sheet of paper left. There were piles of straw against the wooden doors here and there, which seemed to bear out the rumor that the Japanese were prepared to burn the city if the Chinese attacked it again.

Anyone in whose house a gun was found was shot. Shou-yu had a gun in his office because he was in demand as a starter for athletic events. There was a tense moment when the gun was found by the mopping up party. His secretary explained that Mr. Chi was a well-known starter. Fortunately all the bullets found were blanks, so he got away with having the gun confiscated.

All this time I was scouting for a way to go south. British ships were still running, but were booked far ahead. It must have been about

August 25 when I dropped in at a steamship office (I forget which one) expecting the usual brush-off, but hoping for a miracle. I got one.

"We are sending a ship off schedule this evening to evacuate foreigners from Tsingtao. If you can be ready by five o'clock you can take it as far as Chefoo."

I had already put all the money I could lay hands on into travelers' checks, so I paid for a ticket on the spot.

At five o'clock, after a crazy few hours, I reached the wharf from which a launch would leave to take me to the ship at Tangku. As the only foreign passenger, I would have a launch all to myself. I protested that the one for Chinese was overloaded, and that some of them could just as well come with me.

"Sorry, ma'am. This is one rule we never break."

When the heavily loaded launch pulled away before mine, the agent mopped his brow and said, "That's a relief. We have some number one Chinese there, and the Japanese are after them."

We got to the ship about nine o'clock, ahead of the Chinese passengers. When they arrived they came aboard with a general, jovial air of "Thank God!" Once on a British ship, they were out of the country, and safe. I learned that one of them was the editor of *Yi Shih Pao*, the newspaper that I had found counterfeited in the Chinese city. Finding that his own reputation was being used to undo his work, he had realized that there was no future for him in North China.

After a good sleep, we had several hours on a calm, sparkling sea to Chefoo. There was hot discussion of whether it was better to get off at Chefoo, with the probablity of waiting several days for a bus, or to risk going on to Tsingtao, from where there should be a train to Tsinan. There was no way of knowing whether fighting had broken out in Tsingtao. If it had, there would be no more trains, and the ship would have to be filled with evacuees. From Chefoo there might be a bus to Weihsien, and train from there to Tsinan, but there was a rumor that the buses had been taken over by the military.

The captain strongly discouraged going to Tsingtao. The shipping company compradore at Chefoo gave assurance of at least one bus a day, but said that Tsingtao would probably be quiet for at least one more day. Most people took a chance on Tsingtao, but I and several others adhered to the original plan.

As a foreigner, I was taken at once to the jetty, and had only to show my passport. The Chinese had to wait in sampans for up to two hours for customs examination. I got the name of a hotel and went ahead to reserve rooms. Because of the rush of people to the south, the price of lodging had trebled, but still I got the best rooms for two *k'uai* each.

The hotel clerk assured us that there were always several buses the morning after a ship came in. If we were at the station by three in the morning we should get on all right. We did so, and found seven people in line ahead of us. We chose our stoutest fellow to hold our place in line. About seven o'clock, just as he reached the window, the sale of tickets was stopped. The few people ahead of us had bought large numbers of tickets.

We learned that a person who came too late to get tickets honestly would slip a couple of dollars to someone at the head of the line to get them for him. We were furious, and it must have showed, as whenever I approached the station master he took refuge in his inner sanctum. It seemed that, being eighth in line, with twenty buses going, we should have had places. We learned that six buses had been sold as express buses at half again the usual fare, and that express tickets had been bought in the office without standing in line.

Our stout fellow held his place in line while the rest of us asserted ourselves rather freely in other parts of the station. We were offered a chance to ride in an open lorry at the regular bus fare. We were going to accept, but just then they decided to send two more buses, and we got on one of them.

One of the most vexing questions in traveling at such a time is how much baggage one can take. I had limited myself to what I could carry, and had even left my typewriter behind (knowing that Wally had one) in order to bring a few winter clothes. I saw that some people had piles of luggage.

About two in the afternoon it began to pour. When we came to a roadside bus stop with a covered shed the attendant said that all traffic must stop because the unpaved road was of military importance and must not be rutted. The baggage from the top of the bus was taken into the shed, and we stood there until the next day. The rain continued. When it dripped on my head some kind soul emptied his cigarette tin into his pocket and gave me the can to catch the drip.

The people from the nearest village brought us what they could: teakettles of boiled water and cups we could share to drink it, hard-boiled eggs and mooncakes. I took water in my cigarette tin rather than use their cups.

At nine in the morning we had permission to proceed. It was a beautiful drive, eastward along the picturesque coast of Shantung, and then south through rich farmland to Weihsien. There we got a train for Tsinan, arriving in the evening. The next train for Nanking would be at five in the morning. It was impossible to look for any comfort among the hordes of people in the station and the town. We made a pile of our luggage and slept on it as best we might. People of all kinds and conditions swirled around us as we tried to doze.

On the train the next morning we found the people who had gone on to Tsingtao. They had won their bet, and had reached this point as soon as we did and much more comfortably.

At P'uk'ou, where the railroad ended across from Nanking, we were too late for the last ferry boat. People were sleeping all over the streets, having come across the river to escape the night bombing of Nanking. The owner of a little waterfront hotel said a group of us could use his own room, as he had to deal with the crowds all night. Having only one bed, we took turns napping and playing cards.

During the night the sirens blew for an air raid. Six soldiers appeared to "protect" the foreigner, and stayed close to me until the clear signal. Perhaps they were really protecting against me.

At six o'clock we took the first ferry to Nanking. My companions left me, and I took rickshaw to the National Epidemic Prevention Bureau, where Wally had been staying with his twin brother, Bill. The policeman at the gate said that the place had been bombed and nobody lived there anymore.

Frantically I searched my purse for a slip of paper with the address of Eldest Brother Frank: 35 Ling Yuan. The puller was reluctant to take me so far, but I promised to pay him well. We went outside the city to what was evidently a very high-class area, but could not find number 35. Around and around we went, and at last spied a tiny, foreign-style bungalow between two impressive mansions.

My pounding on the gate was answered by a servant who was sure that a foreign lady could have no business there at that hour of the morning. I convinced him that I had to see Liu Hsing-hwa, and he took me to the house where men were sleeping all over the floor. They readily understood who I was and called Wally. He came out, rubbing his eyes and saying sleepily, "What are you doing here? I thought you'd be at least a week on the way."

Chapter 6

I can best convey the flavor of the next few weeks by quoting from the long letters and journal entries I wrote at the time.

Letter, Nanking, September 6, 1937
Dear Folks,

When I got here, August 28, Wally's teaching job in Kwangsi was still hanging fire. The day I came he was offered a job editing an English language journal for the New Life Movement (a social reform organization dreamed up by Chiang Kai-shek). English editorial work is his second choice after teaching, so he accepted and began working. Four days later came a contract from Kwangsi, but he now felt committed to the new job, so here we shall stay.

You can't do yourself or anyone else any good by shutting your eyes to the fact that you are engaged in a struggle for life. I might add that other nations interested in international law and the sanctity of treaties aren't gaining anything by ignoring the fact that China is fighting their war for them, and that if she loses they will have to fight it for themselves later.

I think the question of American or European intervention in this war should be divorced entirely from the question of protecting the lives and property of their nationals (which seems to be their only concern), and should rest on the international obligations they have assumed in the various peace pacts they have signed, and on a consideration of what the issues involved mean for civilization. If China is subjugated by Japan it means, clearly and simply, the loss of any validity that international law may still retain, the practical scrapping of every international agreement, and the deliverance of the world to the predatory powers. Will Italy and Germany hold back from their ambitions when encouraged by one more example of unrestrained aggresssion?

The League of Nations was supposed to handle such situations, but it has no teeth because no nation has been willing to yield any real power to it.

I'm not arguing for military intervention, only that my country should not continue to supply Japan with the aviation gasoline and scrap metal without which she could not do what she is doing to China.

For the present I am vegetating here, building up after the hectic weeks in Tientsin. I am very thin. I haven't had the let-down that I expected. I just stay on the place, look at the hills without wanting to climb them, putter in the garden, and spend endless hours studying Chinese and making, by hand, some of the clothes we'll need for winter. I should be writing up my experiences for an American magazine.

When I came the household consisted of Frank (eldest brother, who owns the house), Bill (Wally's twin brother, who moved here when a bomb fell on his laboratory), Wally, and several men taking refuge from dangerous spots in town. Phoebe had taken the children to Kuling. All the servants but one had gone. The one man was doing the cooking, marketing and washing, and threatening to leave. Soon he did leave, and I had three days of being alone here all day, getting myself cold lunches because no one thought I should tackle the smoky mysteries of the coal ball stove. I took the chance to clean the kitchen, or at least try to.

At last a she-cousin who lived alone with a little servant girl in the city moved out here for safety, and a boy with some gumption from a hut in the valley near by came to help. The boy cleans and goes to market. Cousin cooks, with the help of the boy and the maid, and does some washing. The little girl does the washing and a lot of this and that, I do the ironing, with a charcoal iron, and most of the mending. Ironing is more of a job than you might think, as the men wear khaki suits that have to be washed daily. Before the war they wore white duck in summer, but that's forbidden now because of air raids.

During the servantless era all the unrelated men left us, so now we're only family. Cousin speaks Hupeh dialect, but we get along.

Wally worked like a demon to write the copy for the first issue of his newsletter, but when he presented it to Colonel Huang (Madame Chiang's chief lackey, who is in charge of the New Life Movement), the colonel said he had decided they couldn't afford a newsletter. So Wally refused the Kwangsi job in vain, and is stuck doing odd jobs in an organization he doesn't like.

I had a letter from Emily yesterday. She said that when you saw her name and mine among the survivors of the Tientsin bombing you concluded that the children must be dead. That just goes to show the hopelessness of trying to give accurate impressions of a situation. When we knew that the United Press was sending out the names we supposed that would put your minds at rest. Please take my word for it that things always sound worse than they are.

Yesterday there were two raids. There didn't seem to be any legitimate objective. They seemed deliberately to bomb the most densely populated areas. So much of what they do is like that—pure barbarism with no military advantage. I suppose this is in line with their announced intention to wipe out the city of Nanking.

I may be able to get a job doing the English radio news every evening. We've had some whose voices didn't carry and who couldn't pronounce the names. The one we have now makes such mistakes as referring to a bomb weighing twenty-five kilometers.

Wally has been able to get his ancient typewriter overhauled so it's working well now.

Love to all,

Journal, Nanking, October 15, 1937

Yesterday was my birthday, and a beautiful day, so of course we had alarms off and on all day. They seem determined to make as much hay of us as they can when the sun shines. Every time I thought I might have time for a bath the sirens came again. I gave up hope of doing anything but sit in the gazebo with my flash cards and wait for the planes.

As I sat alternately dozing and shuffling the cards, a distant sound of bombers drew my attention. Bombers make a sound different from fighter planes, a deep, throbbing hung-hung-hung.

I gathered my bag of precious things and went across the garden to a six-foot trench roofed over with planks, and with the displaced earth piled over the top. This is the common type of dugout, cheap to build and adequate against anything but a direct hit—something you don't worry about because it would be as rare as a lottery prize, and if you did get one you'd never know it.

Cousin and the little maid came from the house. The girl was quiet, her bright, darting eyes showing nervousness. Cousin seemed very calm as her fingers flew, shelling peas. I sat where there was enough light for my flash cards.

The sound came closer. I peered out and saw seven bombers, each accompanied by two fighters, just over the Purple Mountain, gleaming in the afternoon sun. The sirens came on again, warbling in wild disharmony, the urgent call.

Ten fighters swept up from the south. The Japanese fighters turned to face them. The sky was full of the crescendoes of swift machines, circling, climbing, diving and firing machine guns. Spent bullets fell, knocking leaves off the trees above us. One plane grew a long, black tail and headed for the ground as a parachute opened. I had no way to know whether it was friend or foe.

The fighters drew away as the bombers went over the city, where the anti-aircraft guns, known as Archie, have to be free to fire without fear of hitting our own planes. The bombers went on, with white puffs of Archie fire around them, and the sound of many explosions showed that they were doing the work they came to do. Half an hour later the clear signal sounded, a sustained note of the siren. Whatever was going to happen had happened.

Then I had the job of waiting for Wally to come home. In my eight months of marriage I have spent a lot of time waiting anxiously to hear from him, and he from me.

At last a normal banging on the gate.

"What took you so long?"

"There were two bombs in my compound. No one hurt, but it was a mess. Then on my way home the road was blocked and I had to go a long way around."

He fished in his pocket and brought out a letter from Mother, the first since the war began. My long letter about the bombing of Tientsin had reached home. Mother assured me of a welcome if I should ever wish to come home, but respected my wish to stay with my husband. She had always respected my judgment, and wouldn't change now. I kissed the letter and put it in the bag of precious things that I kept with me at all times.

Cousin produced a quick meal. Bill came home, bringing a friend whose home had been bombed. Everyone went to bed early.

I dreamed that I was on a ship pitching in a heavy sea while the foghorn blew incessantly. I tried to control my stomach as I was flung up and down by the ship's motion. At last it dawned on me that what I heard was not a foghorn, but a siren. I grabbed Wally. "Wake up! There's an alarm!"

"I've been shaking you for the last five minutes."

It was a beautiful, clear night. We sat on top of the dugout looking at the moon and listening for the planes, which never came.

Life went on. I enjoyed the garden and the sense of respite and the brilliant fall sunshine. I was gathering strength for the ordeals that I knew would come.

One evening the phone rang. "This is Hall Paxton at the American Embassy. We have a boat ticket to Hankow for you tomorrow morning."

"You have a *what*?

"A boat ticket to Hankow. The Japanese have notified all the embassies that they are going to destroy Nanking in the last three days of this week, and they will not be responsible for any foreigners who may be here."

"Well, you can tell the Japanese for me that I have a perfect right to be here, and that they are fully responsible for anything that may happen to me."

"I think I'd like to meet you. I can't force you to go. If you are in town when anything starts, run to the embassy. It will be the safest place."

So a few days later I had lunch at the embassy while bombs reverberated around the city. There I met an American journalist couple named McDaniel who had a Scottie dog with puppies, for which they were desperate to find homes. They somehow got the impression that I would be a responsible owner, so they gave me two puppies, who became our beloved Jeannie and Jackie, enriching and complicating our lives.

The entire diplomatic community except the Americans reacted as I did to the Japanese threat, and the attack was scaled back. The American ambassador, Nelson Johnson, removed such nationals as were willing to go, and steamed several miles up the river in his gunboat. Hall Paxton refused to go. He told me that he and Johnson had not wanted to comply with the Japanese demand, but they were under orders from President Roosevelt to take any means to get Americans out of China.

Life went on tranquilly in the little garden, but the sense of foreboding deepened gradually.

∾

Shanghai fell after bitter resistance. Then for a while we didn't know what to expect.

One night in mid-November, when Wally and I were already in bed, Frank came home and called Wally to talk with him in the other room. When Wally came back to bed he said, "There is an intelligence report that the Japanese have decided to march on Nanking. All dependents of government people who haven't already gone must leave at once. You can go and stay with my family."

"Nonsense! I've told you before that if I can't be with you I'll find some kind of job, and not just roost with your family."

"Well. we don't have to decide tonight, but think about it."

The next day Cousin was busy airing and packing things. Frank came home at mid-morning and sat at the dining table, peeling pears and offering them to me.

"I want you to understand about this evacuation thing," he said. "When the time comes for the government to go, all transportation will be commandeered, and there will be no room for you. You have to go first."

"All right," I said, "I'll be reasonable. We can discuss it again in a few weeks."

He arranged for Cousin, the little maid, and our two dogs to leave on a friend's junk at once. The next day he left with his office, and on the following day Wally and I went to the waterfront with the New Life staff to await a ship for which they had obtained tickets. For one reason or another we were there by the river in a pouring rain for forty-eight hours, surrounded by indescribable disorder. Our ship arrived and went on without stopping, already overloaded. Some of our men caught the agent and got our money back.

When a city of a million has been reduced by evacuation to about three hundred thousand, and most of the shops are closed, it seems rather dead. That dormant city was the Nanking I knew. But when the remaining three hundred thousand try to move all at once it is anything but dead. Chaos reigns. Every means of transportation is jammed, rickshaws are raking in the dollars, it takes pull to get a taxi, and people are setting out on foot for who knows where.

At a moment when nothing seemed to be happening for us, Wally and I went to a nearby hotel to get some rest. We were just relaxed when someone came and called us to try to get on a British ship for which we had no tickets. We loaded our things onto a big sampan. Someone said we'd have time to eat, so we dashed to a food vendor. As we swallowed our second bite of lunch someone came running for us. We had to get another sampan. As the crew tried to hoist its sail the rope broke and we went whirling around in mid-stream, bumping into other boats, until it managed to pull alongside another sampan.

The others were going to try to get deck passage, but I knew a British ship would never sell deck to a foreigner. If I couldn't get a ticket, Wally and I would leave our luggage with the others and try to go by train, or walk if we must.

I went straight to the captain on the bridge. He was not happy to learn that another wave of people had swarmed aboard. He was sure he had no place for me, as he had long ago decreed that only ladies could have cabins, and there would be men sleeping all over the public rooms. The weather was too bad for sleeping on deck.

I insisted that all I needed was a place to sit. He protested that I didn't seem to understand what was suitable for a white woman. I asked if it would be more suitable for me to walk to Hankow? He called the chief steward, who checked his chart and found that there was still one man in a cabin, and the other berth in that cabin had been given to a woman. I was in! I paid fifty *k'uai* for first-class passage, and Wally and the others slept down between decks where they had room to stretch out, but the air was terrible.

I hated being so privileged, but since it couldn't be helped I enjoyed it. Wally and some others could come to my cabin for a good wash each day.

In Wuchang I would have to meet my mother-in-law.

Chapter 7

We reached Hankow at noon on November 23, 1937. By the time we took care of one hundred pieces of luggage for our party and got across the river to Wally's home it was four o'clock. Wally's mother, whom I learned to call P'o-p'o, was the only one at home, and she was so flustered that she forgot to set off the firecrackers to welcome the bride. She was a pudgy little person with a warm smile. I made the three bows that Wally had taught me as an acknowledgement of relationship, and she gave me a pure gold ring.

We had to go out again to help supervise the transfer of things to the new office by cart, rickshaw or shoulder pole. There was a spectacular sunset over the Yangtze. The river, which had been rough and gray during our trip, became calm. Junks and sampans floating across the golden reflection of the sunset looked peaceful and romantic. It was lovely, but we'd have liked the bad weather to continue until the evacuation of Nanking could be completed. With the weather clearing, more Japanese pilots would be out bombing ships.

When we got back to the house we were greeted by a great salvo of firecrackers. Then sirens sounded and I learned the local air raid routine. We brought in all white clothes from the line (bamboo poles laid between two upstairs galleries), loosened the window fastenings to make the house more resistant to vibration, and sat on the first floor. There was no dugout, as the water table is too near the surface to permit digging trenches. I sat by the fire scribbling Chinese characters. After a while Wally's father offered to help me. He had lots of time, and would like to give me Chinese lessons. I didn't know just how to handle this, as he spoke a broad Hupeh dialect, not what I wanted to learn.

Lots of Wally's friends came to dinner. There was a red tablecloth in honor of the bride. P'o-p'o had outdone herself in the kitchen. Trying to be polite, I said "There is too much food," as a guest should do. Everyone laughed and said I was the hostess and should have said "There is no food."

P'o-p'o took me to the kitchen for a cooking lesson. We put a chopped pork mixture between slices of lotus root and fried the sandwich in deep fat. She told me the names of the cooking utensils over and over, and laughed with me over my efforts to learn them. Of course she spoke Hupeh dialect, so much of what I knew was useless with her, and much of what she taught me had to be relearned.

Someone told me that P'o-P'o was pleased with me because I was not "modern." That word (*mo tung* in Chinese) suggests a person who has become so enamored of the Western standard of living that she cannot be satisfied without a flush toilet and all that that implies. She loves to dance and go out, but thinks it beneath her to go to the kitchen. Such people forget that most Chinese, even of high position, live and die without modern conveniences, and that nobody in any country had them a generation ago. They forget their own childhood, and think they are somehow above sharing the makeshifts and inconveniences of the less enlightened.

Hankow and Wuchang were busy places, crossroads for what has been called "the greatest mass migration in history." Wally could scarcely move without meeting people he had known before. Most didn't know whether they would be staying there or moving on to Chungking, Chengtu, Changsha, or even Kweilin, Kweiyang or Kunming. All these names seemed distant and strange. Nobody felt sure of staying anywhere more than a few months.

We saw a lot of wounded soldiers wandering around in padded coats with red crosses on them. Most of them seemed very cheerful. The troops we saw pouring into Nanking when we left there seemed to have high morale.

The junk with Cousin and the puppies arrived in due course, and the puppies made quite a sensation.

The day after they came I felt a cold coming on and decided to stay in bed to head it off. P'o-P'o and Cousin were delighted. They kept coming to assure me that it was perfectly normal not to feel well in the morning, and that it would be all right later. When I still didn't get up in the afternoon they couldn't hide their disappointment. A bride who doesn't function promptly as a baby machine is cause for concern. What, after all, is the whole purpose of marriage?

Frank sent a man to Nanking to get some silver he had hidden there. He found that officers were living in the house, and that the garden had been dug into trenches. Later someone reported that Frank's house and all near it, including President Lin Sen's mansion, had been destroyed, and the forests on the hill cut down, so as not to offer cover to the Japanese, who would be coming from that direction.

Then came the order to leave for Chungking, just one month after leaving Nanking. We left Wuhan on a Chinese ship on December 21, 1937, with the whole New Life staff. The boat was crowded to the gunwales, with people sleeping on every inch of deck. Ch'u Djang (Wally's immediate superior) wangled a sailor's cabin and invited Wally and me to share it: himself on the top bunk, me on the lower, and Wally on a row of suitcases on the floor. The puppies were a problem, but we kept them in a basket except for regular walks on leash. When the deck passengers sat up one could move freely among them, but not when they lay down. The only place where we could let the dogs do their business was under President Lin Sen's official limousine which was chained to the after deck, an elegant machine with only six hundred miles on the odometer.

Unlike the British ship on which we left Nanking, this one had no qualms about taking me any way that was available. I was interested, however, to find that the crew assumed I was Russian, as those were the only white women likely to travel that way.

We should have reached Chungking in five days, but it took six because we were stuck on a sand bar for several hours on Christmas Eve. A British ship passed us, the passengers taking pictures of us as they went by. A little motor boat belonging to the Customs Service went back and forth taking soundings to find out where the water was deep enough for us. They made a map and gave it to the pilot. Then we waited until another Chinese ship came along to pull us free. Because of this delay we had to spend Christmas on board.

That ship took us as far as Ichang, where the big ships from down river have to stop. Further progress was by special, powerful, shallow-draft boats designed to be able to go through the famous gorges, with their rapids and rocks and whirlpools. People were pouring into Ichang on big ships and leaving on little ones, with the result that the town was jammed. It took us eighteen days to get away.

After a couple of nights on the pews of a church we managed to find a tiny hotel room with simple meals available. It was mid-winter, and we had a charcoal brazier, made of the lower part of a Standard Oil tin supported by a wooden frame, like those that provide winter heat for most of southern China. I soon learned that I am extremely sensitive to carbon monoxide. Long before other people began to feel the effects, I would get a headache and have to set the fire outdoors. The buildings were drafty enough so that most people could tolerate the charcoal fire longer than I, but a doctor told me later that everyone operated at two-thirds efficiency in winter because of the accumulation of carbon monoxide in the blood.

A new thing for us in Ichang was citrus fruit, tree-ripened and delicious, in great variety from tiny tangerines to huge oranges and pomeloes, and some kinds that were just for fragrance, not for eating.

Aside from our own group, Wally kept finding old friends among the crowd, so we had a lively social life as the days dragged on, meeting in little groups in restaurants or anywhere where anyone had found a niche. Boat after boat left without us.

One night we had a group boiling water chestnuts on our charcoal fire when a friend came under our balcony and shouted that we must go. After so many false alarms I just sat on the bed and said, "I shan't stir a step. I don't believe it."

Someone came up and gave us our tickets, and within an hour we were on board, dogs and all, in a twelve-berth cabin with sixteen people in it. We got lower berths opposite each other, so it wasn't bad. Wally wanted to get me a first-class cabin, but I was glad he didn't. I stand third-class travel at least as well as he does, and it's really all we could afford. His expenses were paid by the Association, but mine weren't.

The only place where we could let the dogs out was at the bow, in front of all the deck clutter, which was also the best place to admire the scenery. We had looked forward to the Yangtze gorges, but this was December. Fog and drizzle usually obscured the view. The grandest part didn't take my eye as much as the approach through green, ledgy hills and limestone cliffs rising tier after tier, and grassy spots high up with old trees and little huts or temples that seemed to have grown there.

The river was very narrow and swift in the gorges, and reasonably deep. Only specially built ships could go there; all the usual ideal of a ship cutting the water smoothly was sacrificed to the necessity for shallow draft. They could draw not more than seven feet. Blunt-bowed and broad of beam, and driven against the current by powerful engines, they churned the water into hurricane fury on either side, tossing the junks and sampans in their wake like waterbugs. In those days there were dangerous rocks and whirlpools (later removed by the Communist government) so that it was not safe to navigate at night. Every evening we tied up, and often we could take the dogs ashore.

After the gorges the hills became smaller and the country greener. Farmers were raising a quick crop on a riverbed that would be submerged in spring. The fields were neat and attractive. As the hills got smaller and greener we began to see houses that were white and half-timbered instead of earth-colored. There were many grand, old trees.

On January 17, 1938 we reached Chungking.

∾

The Nationalist Government, or Kuomintang (KMT), chose as its wartime capital a city so remote and inaccessible as to be probably out of reach of the Japanese army, and perhaps even their bombers. Chungking had long been known, to those few hardy enough to go there, as a densely-populated city on the tongue of land where the Kialing River (Jah-ling) joins what the world calls the Yangtze (Son of the Sea). In these upper reaches it is called the River of Golden Sands because of the grains of gold that may be found by people patiently washing the sand of the river bottom in winter.

Tumbling down from Tibet, fed by the spring and summer snow melt, it is already a boisterous river with two thousand miles yet to go to reach the sea. Special, shallow-draft ships ply the turbulent channel, traveling only by day because of the many traps the river sets for them. In winter the wide, bare, sandy river bottom is exposed, with the still-powerful river winding through it.

The two swift rivers have carved a way through rugged hills, so that one must climb four hundred eighty ancient stone steps from the river to the city, whether you come by boat or by the motor road from the south (which stops across the river). The first sight of Chungking is of this enormous, wide stairway reaching skyward, bustling with people who walk, carry loads hanging from shoulder poles, or ride in bamboo sedan chairs borne on the shoulders of chanting carriers. Clinging to the cliff on either side are wood-and-bamboo huts, two or three stories high, propped up with poles, and sheltering a swarm of humanity living their lives in defiance of gravity and poverty.

The land along the wall, with its great view of the hills across the river, is the choicest real estate in the city. Both the Methodist Mission and the building we occupied for more than a year are there. The Canadian Mission and the foreigner's summer houses are across the river.

Within the city narrow old streets, some only an arm-span across, wind and climb, usually in the form of stairs. One motor road was being

49

built when we came, cutting through the old houses and making the broad loops by which motor traffic moves upward. On this road rickshaws could be used, though they were mankillers on the upgrade and perilous on the down. Unless one had a car one could go farther in five minutes by the stairs than in half an hour on the road. Cars, of course, were used only by the very rich or the very powerful.

The restricted area between the rivers had always been crowded. Now it was packed with people, cooking and heating with charcoal or smoky coal, and awaiting the bombs that would inevitably fall among them. The air was heavy and murky, and everyone coughed. Coming down from a visit to the hills across the river, I saw what looked like a great, yellow muffin covering the city. The word *smog* had not been invented.

More than three hundred years ago a mad general massacred the population of Szechuan province, saying, "God has done everything for man, but man has done nothing for God, therefore man should be killed." This left a very rich province empty, and it was filled by people from Hunan, who took over everything, becoming fiercely clannish and territorial and resisting all ties with the outside world.

It was into this inhospitable setting that Chiang Kai-shek brought his government and the thousands of refugees who poured up the river as the war went on. Lest they be trapped in their mountain retreat, the government set about opening lines of communication with the outside world. There was soon regular air service to Hankow, Hong Kong and other places. Roads to Chengtu, Kweiyang, Kunming, and other cities became high-priority projects. These roads had to be used before they were finished, as soon as a narrow track was blasted out of a cliff. We heard hair-raising accounts of driving around perilous switchbacks, waiting for rocks to be removed from the next curve, and looking at the remains of cars and trucks far below. As it became clear that other ways would be blocked, intensive work was begun on the Burma Road, from Kunming to Rangoon, built by thousands of people with baskets and shoulder poles.

In Chungking every aspect of Nationalist China was concentrated: Corrupt, cynical, power-hungry people, and others trying to salvage some good out of the mess.

This was the milieu in which Wally and I would survive for nearly two years.

Chapter 8

Journal, our own apartment in Chungking, February 8, 1938

We reached Chungking in the afternoon of January 17, expecting to camp out at New Life Headquarters until we could find a place of our own, but they had already found a place where Wally and I could camp by ourselves. My first misgiving came when I learned that the house was on White Elephant street, but I was so eager for a place where I could do things for myself that I didn't realize at first what a white elephant we had.

The room we were to use was on the third floor of an old building with high ceilings and huge rooms. Judging by the dust, it must have been empty for years. Our room was supposed to have been cleaned for us, but the too-wet mop had only turned the dirt on the floor into mud, which wasn't dry yet. We had one canvas cot with us, which I used, and the man in charge lent us one of the crude wooden bunks he had bought. That was all the furniture we had the first night, but at least we could lay things on the upper bunk and not put them on the muddy floor. All our luggage except the knapsack and bedding roll was still at headquarters. We had a thermos and a little earthen cooking bowl. We sent a servant from headquarters to buy us a water pail, a small wooden tub, an earthen charcoal stove (like a flower pot), charcoal and kindling, and few other things for which we couldn't wait.

The urgency for having all that came from the fact that during the landing the puppies had been kept in their basket too long, and had to have a bath. That was a project in itself.

With great optimism I set out the next morning to do my own cooking and make the place fit to live in. There were deep windowsills to work on, but what a scrubbing it took to make them fit to use, and how much too high they were for me!

Wally ran out in the morning to buy food. With only one cooking bowl it had to be a one-dish meal. Until we found a place to buy earthenware, our menu was like this: morning, sesame cakes from a vendor; noon, a grand Irish stew with lots of meat and vegetables; evening, the remains of the stew plus water, eggs and noodles. It may sound monotonous, but we loved it after all the boats and hotels.

When it was too hard to cook at home, or when Wally found some old friend he wanted to entertain, we went out to eat. Being unacccustomed to hot pepper, I had to learn to pick my way warily through the fiery Szechuan menu.

We gradually accumulated things to make the work easier: a big knife so I didn't have to worry things apart with a paring knife, more bowls so we didn't have to eat up one dish before cooking another, lids to protect things from rats, a nice little brass frying pan. The more varied menu was a cause for joy. We had pork shreds fried with bamboo shoots, and stir-fried cabbage.

Cooking was only one of the problems. We were on the third floor, and I had to run down to a dirty little yard every time the dogs needed to go out. For a privy it was down to the yard and up two long flights of stairs to the back part of the building, which was meant for kitchen and servants' quarters. I learned to time my own excursions to coincide with the dogs'. I took their chains along and tied them to the stairs while I made my trip. Later we bought a five-cent piece of earthenware to use for a night pot.

I used too much energy cleaning at first, scrubbing with inadequate materials and limited water the three windowsills where I worked and the spot on the floor where I fed the dogs. If I'd known I'd be there three weeks, I'd probably have scrubbed the whole floor, but I'm glad I didn't. With a good daily sweeping it gradually improved, and I was pushing myself too hard. The first two or three days I'd burst into tears over nothing, which is not like me. Wally made me take a rest, and he came home and cooked himself, but he got so tired I wouldn't let him do it anymore. As we got better organized it became easier.

The sense of strain and the emotional instability were probably signs of early pregnancy, but I'm not sure yet.

In choosing a house we had to have a place to let the dogs out. We settled on a most individual sort of crow's nest, which is where we are living now. It's a huge ancestral hall, occupying the entire fourth floor of one wing of an apartment building. The landlord was moving his ancestral tablets to safety in the country. He built wooden partitions to suit us, placed with reference to four big, red pillars. There are red roof beams with ornate gilding, real palace style. The floor is concrete, and there are casement windows all around, twenty-two in all, facing the four winds. There is a sizable flat roof where the dogs can run.

We had to pay three months' rent in advance at $20 per month. This, together with electrical installation and necessary equipment, left us pretty well strapped. The landlord is letting us use quite a bit of furniture: two carved rosewood tables, six little tea tables, and eleven formal chairs to go with them along the wall. It suits the place very well. The ancestral shrine makes a fine cupboard.

We have bought a bed for $8.50, cheap bamboo furniture for the kitchen and amah, two big water jars (as water has to be carried in) and lots of necessary little things. Wally had no idea how many things are needed for the simplest housekeeping. Anyway, now that we have a place and an amah, I can try to get some private pupils to get us back on our feet.

When we agreed to take this place the landlord said the work would be done in five days. On the fifth day I went to look, and found one man sawing logs into boards by hand in the yard. Wally talked to the owner, and he put a crew to work, promising to have it done in four days more. After three days I went and found the key planks in place and the work progressing nicely, but they were doing such a beautiful job, planing and tonguing and grooving with hand tools,and fitting everything together exquisitely without nails, that I could see it would take at least a week more. Within that week the Chinese New Year holidays intervened, when no work can be done, so we were in the White Elephant for three weeks.

Saturday, February 5th, while the men were still working on the living room partition, we moved in. What fun to sleep in a real bed, and not have to run downstairs to let the dogs out!

Phoebe's amah recommended an amah for us. They said she was a number one maid and wouldn't wash clothes or empty slop jars or scrub floors. I said in my little place I had to have one person who would do everything. She said she would. She arrived in the middle of Sunday afternoon, and I told her to start dusting. She spent the rest of the day polishing the intricacies of one carved chair, but never touched the dust of ages on the windowsills. The next day, having seen that it would take several days to clean the place, she brought a stupid-looking slattern to take her place while she went to the bedside of her dying mother. When her mother was dead, she would return.

"No, you don't," I thought, and set the other one to dusting. She covered the ground, after a fashion, but she served burned rice and awful food just as Wally had to go back to the office. The supper, which appeared about nine o'clock, was just as bad.

This morning I said she should just clean, and I would cook. Her zeal for cleaning has evaporated. Every time I turn my back she sits down. I point out places she hasn't touched, and she does just what I show her and sits down again. And stupid! I've never seen anything like it. This evening we'll send her packing whether we have anyone else or not.

Workmen came yesterday and built a stove of old stone and bricks, covered with chocolate-colored mud. Today they frosted it with a layer of white plaster icing, like a monster chocolate cake for our wedding anniversary, which is today. Until it's dry I'll still use my little charcoal stove, like a flower pot with a grate in it, set out in the hall or on the porch. Tonight we'll have ox tongue, and the soup from it, and pork with bamboo, and a green vegetable, all cooked with my lily-white hands.

Journal, Chungking, February 10, 1938

That evening the friends through whom we heard about this place came in and found me cooking. They took one look at the stupid face and slovenly clothes of the slattern, and said that their amah *wanted to send us a friend of hers.*

Bright and early the next morning she appeared, a tall, strong woman who is clean and neat, and seems to know what needs to be done without being told. We call her Chiang Sao. She doesn't always understand me, as the Szechuan dialect is different, but we get along well.

Chapter 9

Journal, Chungking, April 6, 1938

I now have several private pupils. The best is a class of three fellows from the Ministry of Foreign Affairs who want to brush up their French. They are doing nice work, and they pay $22.50 each a month, which helps a lot.

The others are all English lessons. I trade English for Chinese with a young man from Peiping whose Mandarin is pure and clear. He is very patient about making me repeat and repeat. We are using the mass education primers (Jimmy Yen's thousand character course).

I had planned to go to language school last summer, but now I'll just have to pick it up any way I can. It's an easy language to start, but hard to master.

I must tell about my little beggar. Szechuan swarms with homeless children, left over from the famine two years ago and from numerous warlord struggles, as well as from the grinding poverty of the lower classes. This is naturally one of the richest provinces of China, but it is also known as one of the most corrupt, so that here one sees the sharpest contrast between great wealth and indescribable poverty. The oppression of the people by extortionate taxes is called "scraping the earth." They say that in Szechuan the sky is three feet higher than anywhere else because the earth has been scraped so low.

Since the government moved up here there have been great efforts to clear the streets of beggars, even if only by moving them to the country out of sight. An orphanage has been set up for orphans under the age of ten. It can hold one hundred, and won't be nearly enough, but it's better than nothing. The social worker at the Methodist Hospital told me that if I found any wild children she could get them into the orphanage.

One afternoon I saw an especially cute and pathetic-looking child, clad in pitiful rags. For warmth she had only half a gunny sack clutched around her shoulders. She had a broken bowl and only one chopstick. She moved from one shop front to another, standing mutely before each one and moving on without asking for anything, as if she had been rebuffed so often that she couldn't bear to ask again. Somebody threw her half a bun.

After watching her for a while, I decided to try to take her to the hospital. I asked her if she had parents. She said no. I asked if she would like to go to where she would have food and clothes. She didn't seem to understand. Thinking my northern Chinese was at fault, I asked a passing woman to explain to her. Her face lighted up with incredulous wonder.

When we reached the hospital it was after five, and everyone who could help was gone. I didn't see how I could turn her loose again after getting her hopes up. I saw no choice but to take her home. I'm not sorry I had the experience, though Wally said it was pretty stupid. I could have given her twenty cents and told her to meet me the next day.

I was uneasy about what Chiang Sao would say to such goings on, but she was incredible. When she opened the door for us I said, "This child wants a bath and food." As calmly as if I had asked for a cup of tea, she said, "Right away. There's hot water ready."

Before I could get into old clothes she had the child kneeling by a tub on the flat roof, while she scrubbed the hair and combed hundreds of lice out of it with the dogs' fine-tooth comb. I would have preferred to cut and burn the hair first, but her way was all right. I did a rude haircut later.

Wally came home while we were working on the lice. He took one look and went out for dinner, saying he couldn't eat in the house with such a mess. He sent the gateman to buy some second-hand clothes.

When we were satisfied with the head we changed the water and had the child strip for a bath. To our surprise it was a boy. The long hair had fooled me. He was a nice little fellow and tried to help in every way he could. He wanted to bathe himself, and had a very good idea of how to do it. I scrubbed a good deal, too, as he could scarcely cope with some of the accumulations. When we were through he rinsed the washcloth and hung it over the edge of the tub, saying, "That's better!"

I gave him a warm, old bathrobe that could be washed, and set a chair for him in the hall, where Chiang Sao gave him a bowl of rice with vegetables. He ate neatly, refused a second bowl with thanks, and sat quietly waiting.

He said his name was Wang Hsin. He was seven years old, which makes him five or six by our reckoning, since Chinese babies are a year old when they are born and gain another year at New Year. He thought his father was a cook in another city. His mother had died in the famine. His older sister had cared for him until she, also, died. He had lost track of his younger brother.

I thought with admiration of his mother, who had given him such good home training that it still showed after a year on the street.

The smallest clothes the gateman could find were too big. We hastily shortened the sleeves so he could wear them. Shy as he was, he smiled when he put on faded but presentable cotton trousers, jacket and padded coat. He slept in the open, with the bathrobe for a bed and something rolled up for a pillow. It seems Spartan, but must have been better than the street.

In the morning, bright and early, he was helping Chiang Sao to pluck a chicken. I dumped everything we had used with him into the tub with a solution of potassium permanganate (cheaper than Lysol) and told Chiang Sao to wash them when she had time, and to wipe down the area where we had worked with a similar solution. Then we went to the hospital, where the social worker took charge of the boy.

Later that day some peculiar sensations caused me to inspect my under-pinnings. When I showed Chiang Sao what I found she made me change everything, sponge myself with Lysol, and give her my clothes to sterilize by ironing. My mother told me that clean people don't have lice. The truth is that clean people don't keep them long.

A few days ago I went with the social worker to visit the orphanage. Wang Hsin came running and bowed over and over, beaming radiantly. He called a younger boy and said this was his friend from the street. He had led a teacher to find this little one. It was wonderful to see these children, none more than a few days or weeks from beggardom. Some were still pale and weak, but they all beamed. They have a little schooling, and are taught manners and practical skills, but the place is very inadequate, and funds insufficient. They wear straw sandals, and some have to sleep four to a bed, but the staff tries hard. Dr. Ruth Hemenway is trying to arrange for the Methodist hospital to give the necessary medical care.

I guess I haven't written anything about Dr. Ruth, who is my doctor now. I am definitely pregnant, and she is my mentor.

I have just seen an open letter from George Fitch of the Nanking YMCA, who was the director of the attempted safety zone for women when the city fell. His account of events after the occupation by the Japanese is harrowing in the extreme. Every day saw mass executions of hundreds of civilians, and countless rapes and casual murders. Disarmed soldiers and any young men of military age were imprisoned and offered amnesty if they would volunteer for labor. When they did, they were roped together in groups of one hundred and used for bayonet practice. Theft of cars and trucks became so general that the Japanese embassy (nice people but powerless against the military) had to appeal to the Safety Zone officials to lend them cars for necessary errands. Some Americans had to spend all their time riding on rice and coal trucks to keep them from being taken.

I can't begin to give an idea of the enormity of the story. It was not polished writing, but seemed a sane and restrained account of authenticated facts.

Letter, 13 Hsuang Hang-tze, San P'ai Fang, Chungking, Szechuan, China, undated, summer 1938

Dear Mother,

You may not think this paper looks nice. There was an awful storm last night. All the dirt from between the roof tiles, quarts and quarts of it, blew down into our rooms, and then it rained torrents, and the roof leaked streams. I should have thought of my writing table first, as it has leaked there before, but I was so busy dashing from one rescue to another that I didn't get there until my little stock of paper, my notebooks, and a book belonging to Dr. Hemenway were a mess. I hope I never see the like again.

I could feel the dirt hitting my face like hard rain, and it was nasty dirt that smeared unless brushed off very lightly. When we got things covered with anything we could find we spent our time sweeping up the drifts from the floor. Chiang Sao was busy bailing out the lakes in her part of the house, where it leaked even worse. When it seemed to be over I pulled the filthy sheets from the bed and fixed it so we could sleep. Then in a couple of hours it began all over again, rain worse than ever but not much dirt.

It certainly was a job to get cleaned up this morning. Chiang Sao proved both valiant and resourceful.

A few days ago she had a nasty-looking eye and an awful headache. I sent her to the eye clinic, which was crowded that day. Someone told her she only had a cold and sent her home. I wasn't convinced. I went with her to the head ophthalmologist and stayed to make sure she actually got to see him. He called it advanced trachoma with corneal ulcers. I have to send her every day for treatment, and treat her myself every three hours. Wally and I have to use zinc sulphate drops in our eyes for prevention. I iron the towels and handkerchiefs myself to sterilize them.

Americans being so ignorant of trachoma, and having an almost super-stitous dread of it, you might be interested to know what the treatment involves. Twice a day I put the preventive zinc sulphate in her good eye and those of the rest of us. As near every three hours as I can I treat the affected eye thus: first a drop of argerol, holding the lids apart with my fingers and forcing her to wink until it is well distributed. Then a quantity of copper sulphate ointment applied under the lids with a cotton swab. She gets the same treatment at the clinic, but of course the doctor is better than I at getting the ointment in properly. The ulcers may require operation later, but they may disappear as the acute condition is cured. We've been doing this for about a week, and I can see marked improvement. The stabbing pains in her head have stopped and she is much more cheerful. Of course you understand that without this care she would soon have been blind. We pay for her treatment, which costs more than her wages. I hope my hands don't get sore, being scrubbed in Lysol five times a day.

There is a boat going by that sounds like bombing planes, a deep, throbbing sound. A couple of times I have roused from a nap thinking, "Bombers close by!" Then I remember that bombers don't come here. I go to the window and see that old boat plowing its way against the current.

Many of the down-river refugees are troubled by the sound of blasting, which is going on all the time as they make tunnels in the solid rock against the time when bombers may be able to come.

I seldom react to it—only now and then when absent-minded.

Love to family and friends,

I wish I could write to all of them

Journal, Chungking, undated, summer, 1938

The vaunted hot weather has come, and it's as bad as they said. Tonight it looks as if we may get a storm to break the heat. We're glad we didn't move. It's true that the roof tiles get hot and radiate, but we're so high above the river, and so open on all sides, that we nearly always have some breeze.

Next day—The storm did not come, and this morning dawned dripping hot. I am now taking my afternoon rest in bed. The sky looks threatening again, and I hope for rain to cool us off.

I continue to be as comfortable as a pregnant woman can expect, but I no longer have the feeling that I am getting something for nothing. Much of the time I feel as if I had been riding a horse with too wide a saddle. I walk more slowly and tire more easily than I did, but I still climb the long streets of stairs with ease.

We wonder how long Hankow can be defended. People are being urged to move out, and every boat is crowded. Bill's office is to come here, but he won't have to live with us. He will have an office dormitory. Wally's parents have gone to Changsha, but now some people think Changsha may fall before Hankow. Brother Frank is in Changsha. Wally's father is not taking it well. Wuhan was badly bombed yesterday.

We have had alarms now and then, but only once did the bombers get anywhere near. We think they must have a base in Hankow before they can bother us much.

I thought that after Hankow fell we'd be pretty well cut off from the world except for air mail, but the road through Yunnan to Burma is being built so fast that I no longer feel so. They are also pushing the construction of a railroad through Yunnan, bucking climate, topography and malignant malaria. It means opening new routes and developing old ones. We'll still be able to get guns and airplane fuel and some basic necessities, and of course the inevitable luxuries: coffee and cigarettes and lipsticks and California lemons and silk stockings for those incredible people who still demand them and have the power to get what they want.

Preparations for the baby are proceeding. I improvised patterns for baby clothes and have been making them of cotton flannel. I made up a way to make infinitely expandable dresses for myself.

Somebody lent me Dr. Emmet Holt's book, The Care and Feeding of Children, *which is the one Mother had for us kids. It was the standard of its day. Mother used to lament that she brought up five of us by it before getting a newer one for Bill. I can certainly understand her feeling when I read such warnings as "no carrots or tomatoes until seven years old."*

I had a wonderful half day in the hills with Ruth Hemenway. I have an invitation to spend a whole day among the tall pines of the second range of hills across the river. Most of the foreigners have gone to their hill bungalows for the summer.

Journal, Chungking, August 12, 1938

Wally recently got into conversation with a man who turned out to be Wan Chia-pao, a former colleague of mine in Tientsin, otherwise known as Ts'ao Yu, China's leading playwright. He is now dean of the National Academy of Dramatic Arts, and he wants me to teach there. I'll have six hours a week, for $72 a month, starting in mid-September and having a month's leave when the baby comes. That will be a godsend, as Irving needs to go to a sanitarium for his TB, and we were wondering how to manage.

Chapter 10

On September 25, 1938, the exact date predicted, labor began with contractions so slight I wouldn't notice them if I was thinking about anything else. I wrote a play by play account for Mother, but never mailed it. I made voluminous journal entries for myself, and so they shall remain. Some things are too intensely personal to share in any detail.

Katie was born at six-thirty Monday morning, September 26, and greeted the world with lusty howls. Ruth said, "Nothing wrong with this baby!" She was the only baby I have ever seen that was pink and beautiful at birth, and not red and wrinkled as normal babies are. I could not know this as a danger sign. Everyone was crazy about her, and she immediately had a proposal of marriage from a friend with a boy baby.

The next day she began to turn blue, and the following Monday she died, gasping for breath. She had seemed normal at first thanks to the fact that the prenatal blood channels, which should close at birth, had remained open for a while. The pulmonary artery was completely blocked. The first "blue baby operation" was years away, and even now (1992) it is doubtful whether such a case could be saved.

Such are the facts. The process by which I became ready to welcome her release is something I can't talk about even now, after fifty years.

When Ruth said, "Your baby's gone," I sobbed, "I'm so glad. Now I want to be busy." She said, "Edith Epstein says they want another English teacher at the Soviet Embassy."

Ruth belonged to the generation of doctors who thought it important for women to stay in bed for two weeks after childbirth. Knowing that the hospital would be bleak for me, she had me taken on a stretcher to her own bed on the upper veranda of the Methodist ladies' house, overlooking the confluence of the Yangtze and Kialing rivers. She set a cot for herself nearby and did much to heal my wounded spirit.

I didn't want to see the body because I wanted to remember my beautiful baby, but when the mission ladies lined a tiny coffin with padded pink satin and decked it with garden flowers I couldn't refuse to look. For a long time the dead look crowded out the beautiful one, but in the end I was glad I had seen it. It helped me to know that what we buried was not Katie really, but only an empty garment she could not use.

As soon as I had recovered enough from the debility caused by staying in bed, I entered on the most interesting part of my checkered career, teaching English to the ambassador and several staff members of the Soviet Embassy.

Letter, Chungking, November 24, 1938
Dear Folks,

I just realized that this is Thanksgiving Day. Funny to think of. I am very busy these days, so that hours to myself are precious. My classes at the National Academy of Dramatic Arts are from three-thirty to five-thirty three days a week. It is an interesting place, though it might better be called the Academy of Propaganda. Ts'ao Yu hates being required to emphasize war propaganda plays instead of dramatic art.

Twice a week I stop at the Soviet Embassy on the way, and every morning from eight to ten I give lessons at the Soviet residential club about fifteen minutes' walk from home. The embassy people keep begging me to take more pupils, but I think I have enough. There's a lot of writing I want to do besides. My income this way is about $150 a month, which makes our joint income very good indeed in these days of salary cuts.

It needs to be, with Wally's tubercular brother Irving still in the Canadian hospital here at $90 a month plus extras. He can leave the hospital in a few days, but must go back every week to have his lung collapsed. He can't think of working this year. He has lung lesions now, as well as pleurisy. We have to find him some place where he can rest.

Wally's parents invested all their savings in real estate in Wuchang, and used to live very well on the rentals, but now, of course, they can't collect any rents, even supposing that the houses are still there and still have any tenants. They are safe in a village in Kweichow, but of course will have to depend on their children for support.

With me earning so well, we can bear our share of such demands, pay off the bill for the baby's special nurse, and save for a rainy day.

Speaking of saving for a rainy day, one of my Russians met that expression in his reading the other day, and wanted to know what it meant. I said he might be sick and need money for doctor or hospital.

"But doctors and hospitals are free."

"You might want to save to send your child to college."

"But all education is free."

"Your house might burn up."

"Then I would be given another."

"You might want to travel."

"If the government allows me to travel, they will pay my expenses."

I felt uneasy at the thought of a culture in which there is no motive for thrift, and in which one may not make one's own decision to travel. I'll tell you more about the embassy people when I know them better.

A refugee relative is with us now. She left Hankow when the Japanese approached, as she did not want to work in occupied territory. She says that although one of Japan's pretexts for the war was the need to expand her markets, they do not export to the territories they have taken, because the puppet currency they use there is no good. They won't even accept it themselves.

Love to all,

Letter, Chungking, Sunday, January 15, 1939
Dear Folks,

The bad thing about bombings is what you will see about them in your paper and be worried. Don't worry. I am usually at the embassy when the alarm comes, and the ambassador and I continue his lesson in the luxurious shelter tunneled in bedrock.

Today for the first time bombers actually got here. I was at the Methodist Mission letting the dogs play in the garden when the Japanese somehow dropped at least twenty bombs on the dry river bottom. Some windows were broken in the house, but it wasn't really close. Now Ruth has gone across the river to attend to the wounded. I almost went along, but there were plenty of nurses, and I wouldn't be able to get back in time to keep Wally from worrying. He was gone for the day, taking comfort supplies to a conscript camp.

Ruth is going to send a Clipper letter to her mother, and she said I could put in a note to be forwarded to you. I won't be extravagant enough to write by Clipper because I think you realize that someone would let you know if anything happened to me. I'd better not impose any more on Ruth's postage.

Love to all,

Journal, Chungking, January 18, 1939

I didn't want to send a graphic account of that bombing to the family, but it was a bad one. We can no longer assume we are safe here. The thirty bombs on the sandbar below our house were doubtless intended for the main business street. Whether the wind deflected the bombs as they fell, so that they passed over our heads and into the river, or whether their aim was that poor, or whatever the reason, the city could have been a real mess if those bombs had landed anywhere else. The only serious damage was at the point between the two rivers, where the land jutted out into the line of flight.

The alarm came while I was at the mission, so they invited me to lunch. Just as the meal was ready I stepped to the door and said, "I hear bombers."

"You think you can tell bombers by the sound? You down-river people are so jittery. Come on. This soup will never be so good again."

Ruth and I were the only ones with experience of bombing. As we started to eat the soup, bombers passed close by, laying their eggs. The windows rattled. Ruth said, "Well, it's done now. We might as well keep on." Then we heard another flight coming. I said, "If they are coming in waves we'd better take shelter." Ruth and I ran to the cave just as another flight passed on the same path. The others stood out where they could watch the bombs fall. They weren't hurt, but they won't do it again. They saw enough to put a little respect into them. I think the real story is that one of the women thought going to the shelter would show a lack of faith in God and the men felt they couldn't go unless she did.

One of them said to me once, "There are guardian angels all around me, and they will turn the bombs aside."

I said, "If they are turned aside from you, may they not fall on somebody else? I don't think faith is supposed to substitute for common sense."

There were about thirty planes carrying small bombs. They wouldn't be able to get here with big ones, as it's a hard trip at best. Our planes went up to intercept them, but couldn't get high enough before they were over the city. We brought down one.

There was a bomb in the compound of the Methodist Girls' Middle School (in a different part of town), and the buildings were rendered unfit for use. No one was hurt unless you count one woman who left for her hill bungalow that afternoon and says she won't come back to town unless it's raining.

About one hundred thousand people left the city in the next three days.

Sometime they will get through again. Perhaps when summer comes, or after Hankow falls, they will come often. We are not worried about ourselves. The chance of being hit is more than that of being struck by lightning, but less than that of being hit by a car in America.

Chapter 11

Letter, Chungking, February 8, 1939

Dear Folks,

I promised to tell you about my work at the Soviet Embassy. After the Academy of Dramatic Arts moved to the country for safety, I was free to go full time to the embassy, fifty minutes' walk from home.

The embassy is a pretentious mansion built by some bygone warlord in a garden on a steep mountainside. The Russians tunneled into the hill behind the house and built an air raid shelter that is nothing short of luxurious. Inside the entrance there are showers for decontamination in case of poison gas. The tunnel, lined with reinforced concrete, has sharp turns and a second opening to prevent concussion in case of a bomb at the entrance. It has its own generator in case of power failure, and a refrigerator always stocked with sandwich makings, fruit and snacks. The main gallery, well lighted, is lined with comfortable wicker chairs, plenty for everyone.

The first time I was in the shelter it wasn't finished. Edith Epstein and I sat on a pile of reinforcing rods and gave a lesson to dear old Ambassador Luganetz, who had a peasant's love of proverbs and sayings. We sat in the dark and taught him the rhyme about hitching your wagon to a star. He memorized it, and often quoted it afterward.

Luganetz would be a chapter all by himself. He was an old visionary, like so many of the early revolutionaries. He commanded an armored train during the revolution, dreaming of a Marxist utopia where life would be good for everyone. One day we met the expression, "throw out the baby with the bathwater." I asked him if he thought that had ever been done in the revolution, and he said yes, in more ways than he liked to think.

He wanted to read the Bible, not for religion, but because you can't understand the English language without it. The same for Mother Goose and our familiar fairy tales. How could one be a diplomat and not understand Humpty-Dumpty, or Cinderella, or David and Goliath? When I went in for his lesson he would often translate some Russian proverb and ask for an English equivalent. When he said, "You can't catch two watermelons with one hand," I replied, "You can't kill two birds with one stone." "Ah," he said, "That is good."

One day there was something about honey, and I said I had been a beekeeper. He said, "In my country we think keeping bees is a job for women or old men. When I am old I will live in a village and keep bees and tell lies to the children about how the revolution could never have succeeded without me."

He never reached that dream. One day when I went for his lesson I was told he wasn't ready. As I waited in a corner of the lounge, he and his wife and a few people I had never seen went out, got in a car, and headed for the airport, where a plane from Moscow had come in the day before. Day after day I was told he didn't have time for his lesson, until at last I was told he had gone to Moscow. Some weeks later we were told that he had been given a vacation at the Black Sea because of his bad back. On the way back the steering gear of the car broke in the Caucasus and the car went over a cliff, killing him and his wife. Of course we couldn't discuss this with the staff, but Edith and I never believed the story. We knew Stalin was "liquidating" too many people for us to believe this was an accident.

All the older men who went through the revolution are being withdrawn from the foreign service, and their places taken by young men who have grown up in the system. Edith, who worked for them in Hankow last year, can see it clearly, and even in the short time I've been here it is noticeable. The older men could discuss what they believed even if you didn't agree with them, but the young ones can neither see nor hear anything that doesn't fit the pattern they have been taught. A few anecdotes may illustrate what I mean.

When Russia invaded Finland I asked the second secretary how this action differed from imperialist war (one of their cardinal sins). He said, "You don't understand. Imperialist wars are fought by capitalist nations." To him it was clear: Anything his country did was not imperialism, but liberation.

My nice young Ukrainian, Mr. Drigalenko, often had trouble with the stupid book he was using. One day he had the story of Robin Hood, with "proud nobles, rich merchants and greedy priests."

He said, "Those adjectives are unnecessary."

"Why?" I asked.

"Because all nobles are proud, all merchants are rich and all priests are greedy."

"I have known many exceptions."

"No. That's the way it is."

Another day his lesson contained the sentence, "The servant stole a great deal of money."

He said, "That is a bad sentence."

"What's bad about it? It has a subject and a predicate."

"I'm not talking subject and predicate. It's a bad sentence."

"Tell me why."

"You must not say such things. It is propaganda against the servant."

"What would you say?"

"I would say, the banker stole a great deal of money."

Another time I thought he made a very good point. The sentence was, "Most of the boys in this class are stupid."

"That is a bad sentence."

"Why?"

"You must not say that."

"How do you know they are not stupid?"

"If they are stupid in this class, you must put them some place where they will not be stupid."

Despite a few bureaucratic inanities, I really like this work. My pupils are mature and intelligent and eager to learn. It's an unusual opportunity to see what makes them tick. They all come from peasant or worker families. Many are grandchildren of serfs. They owe everything to the revolution. At least three of them were once homeless waifs, the "wild children" we used to read about. They were educated by the state, and like everyone else, given all the education they could use and a chance to use it. The only one who seemed to have had any experience of affluence was Mrs. Luganetz, the ambassador's wife, now dead. I gave her French lessons to brush up the French she knew as a child.

They are paid in U.S. dollars. The cook gets $100 a month, and the others up to $150. With exchange at six to one it gives them more than they can possibly spend, even though they pay me out of their own pockets. They have no incentive to save—in fact no concept of saving at all.

Women have theoretically the same status as men. The requirement that everyone must do useful work extends to them. One of the wives is a mechanical engineer, but I don't see any women on the embassy staff, and I doubt if the men help much around the house.

You can't know these people and doubt that they have achieved a lot. I still think any regime based on force and supported by a censored press, and where people can travel only as permitted by the government, carries the seeds of its own destruction. I certainly don't approve of the methods that are used to bring people into line. But whether their system attains stability or not, they have given us a lot to think about.

Letter, Chungking, spring 1939

Dear Mother,

A few days ago one of the famous Szechuan rats stole one of my stockings to make a nest. That's a disaster. I thought of asking you to send some by air express, but then I patched up a pair of old woolen stockings and decided I could get along. It will soon be too warm to need them.

I notice that people do receive their magazines from home, and seem to expect ordinary parcel post to come through in the course of time. If you sent a package now there's a good chance it might get here before next winter. There's no way I can get big enough stockings here. The largest are nine, and I need eleven. No silk, please. Just three pair of lisle knee-highs and a couple of balls of darning cotton to match, and maybe one pair of good lisle long stockings for dress-up.

You'd laugh to see how I'm saving my last bits of darning cotton for such darns as show. Most of our wartime economies don't bother me, but I hate to darn stockings with white thread.

I certainly feel well this year. Last year I coughed my head off, but this year I haven't even had a cold. Maybe it's the halibut oil I'm still taking. I wish Wally would take it too, but he won't unless we have a chance to get some from Hong Kong. He says Irving and I need it more than he does. It costs more than $20 for 5occ here.

Perhaps the fact that I enjoy my work has something to do with my feeling better than when I taught classes. I always got sort of desperate about this time of the year.

Wally's been working his head off on a report of his investigation of conditions in conscript camps. It's been interesting, but depressing. The inhumanity and corruption are beyond belief. He has to finish tonight. I'm going to bed.

Good night, sweet dreams, I love you.

Letter to brother Frank (who was in Peiping, 1922–25), Chungking, March 18, 1939

Dear Frank,

As I sprint around the interminable stone stairways of Chungking, I often imagine that you have come and I am showing you the town. It gives things an extra flavor when I think how different it is from the China you knew. We can't believe it ourselves, when a single issue of the paper may carry the announcement of two new airlines. We now have air service to Hanoi (via Kunming), to Rangoon, and to the Soviet Union, besides Hong Kong, which we had before.

As I wrote Kunming, I realized that this busy hub of Free China travel and transportation is the remote outpost, then called Yunnan-fu, which you visited on your adventurous trip home. Only hardy travelers ever went there in those days.

If you didn't want to fly you could take train from Haiphong to Kunming and come on by bus or truck via Kweiyang.

Unless you had some special connection you'd probably wait days or weeks for a ticket. The bus trip is quite hair-raising, over unfinished mountain roads.

You, with your memories of North China, would surely be amazed at the stairs. It would take you more than five minutes just to climb the stairs from the airport to the road. I'm sure you would walk rather then take a sedan chair, a light bamboo contraption carried on the shoulders of two grunting, sweating human beings. Then you would find yourself on a wide, hard-surfaced motor road, hacked out of the towering cliff and falling away sharply to the river, with two-story wood-and-bamboo shacks somehow propped up by poles against the hill below. I walk along that road every day on my way to the embassy, and I love it because of the sense of openness.

If you came in by ship, as we did, you'd have to climb four hundred eighty old stone steps to get into the city.

There are taxis at the airport, but with gasoline so scarce they cost an awful lot, and are only for big shots. It's quicker to climb the stairs than to go around by the road. We walk nearly everywhere. There are rickshaws in the city, but they can go only on the motor road. The pullers are so small and under-nourished that they can't run like the ones you remember. A level place is just a chance to catch breath before the next climb or descent. Somehow they do manage to pull up some pretty tough hills (nice passengers get out and walk), and they do maintain some sort of control on their mad rushes downhill.

Beggars have been pretty well eliminated, as they don't look nice in a capital city. I don't know what was done with them.

You'd love the fruit and vegetables all year long, including things you've never seen, but I don't think you'd like the climate, dank and unhealthy in winter and dripping hot in summer. Try to come in the spring.

Journal, Chungking, April 21, 1939

We are in the throes of an important decision. Wally has been offered a job as dean of a middle school in Sumatra. In many ways it seems attractive. It's a beautiful place, nice climate, cheap living, with work available for me.

Wally would teach twelve hours a week besides being dean. Teaching is what he likes to do, and he doesn't like his present job at all. And of course, it would be nice to get out of the war.

A few minutes ago I thought I heard a train laboring up a grade, like the one I used to hear struggling up to Waterford at night when I slept on the porch in Northfield. Then it dawned on me that I shouldn't be hearing a train in this part of the world. I went to the window and saw the first of the big summer ships chugging slowly up the Yangtze. The river rises spectacularly at this season, as the snow melts in Tibet. The great rocks across the river look smaller each day, but I hadn't realized the water was high enough to let a ship pass our house.

We've really had a lot of pleasant weather this spring. I hadn't known Chungking could do it. For several weeks I've been having one or two lessons each day in lovely spots in the embassy garden. One of my pupils is good at finding nice places for his lessons. Today we were on a bench facing a gorgeous bank of nasturtiums. It's fun to have my pupil dash off and bring back a snail or something and ask its name in English.

I have a great Chinese teacher. He used to be at the Peiping language school, and he really knows how to teach. I'm learning fast at last. I can read about seven hundred characters, and write about four hundred. I'm just afraid the embassy will ask him to take another pupil at that hour.

It's funny what ideas come into my head when I think of going to Sumatra. Just now I was thinking, if this rotten typewriter ribbon will just hold out until we get there, we can get one as a matter of course, instead of scheming to get one as we do here. I think sometimes of all the stuff we left in Tientsin. I would like to have the pressure cooker and the sewing machine, but it's funny how few things one ever misses.

When people ask what Wally's work is, I just say he is in the New Life Movement Headquarters. If they ask more, I say he is an administrative assistant and does many kinds of work. Then I change the subject. I scarcely know myself what he does because he dislikes it so much he doesn't like to talk about it. I know he has become quite good at drafting documents in classical Chinese (like Latin to us). Once there was a mess of dirty politics and he handed in his resignation so as to be able to speak his mind. The resignation was not accepted, and they promised to give him work that would provide more scope for initiative. He has just done a report on conditions in conscript camps, and the lack of enforcement of the laws against conscripting the sole support of a family, etc. Maybe he was too outspoken, as no more special assignments seem to be coming.

There should be a big field of usefulness for the New Life Movement, but I'm afraid it can't be realized under the present leadership, both immediate and national. It's just window dressing, and we aren't the ballyhoo type.

I just paid $21 to have a pair of shoes made, That's what I get for not having been willing to pay $12 last year.

Wally bought me ten copies of the American Bee Journal *that he found in a second-hand book shop. I had to waste time reading about the latest methods of packing bees for winter in Minnesota.*

Journal, Chungking, April 29, 1939

Just after I wrote the last we read an article in Asia *which made us wonder whether we'd like Sumatra. We've been reading everything we can find, and talking to people who've been there, and I think we'll go. Wally had another letter today urging him to come at once, as the president wants to visit China, and leave Wally in charge while he's gone. He'll probably go as soon as he can get his passport, and I'll follow in two or three months.*

If he leaves first, it would be silly to keep this place just for me. I can get a room with missionaries for $30 a month, and take meals with Edith Epstein at cost. It would come out about the same as we spend here, counting everything. It would seem empty here without Wally.

Ruth has gone to head a hospital in Tzechow, and we are going to give Jackie to her if we can find a way to send him.

Chapter 12

J ournal, Chungking, May 9, 1939

After the failed raid in January the bombers did not reach us again until Wednesday, May 3, 1939, when we suddenly learned that we were not secure in our mountain fastness. I was, of course, in the embassy's luxurious shelter with lights and wicker chairs.

The bombs put the sirens out of commission so we didn't know the raid was over, and stayed in the shelter until about three. Then we went to the top of the garden and saw smoke pouring from the city, but couldn't tell what part because of a hill.

Edith Epstein and Helen Chang and I went to the club room. Our boss, Mr. Skvortzoff, the second secretary, probably realizing that we would be having a bad time, came and kept us company until it seemed safe for us to leave. (Helen is a third English teacher whom I don't think I've ever written about. She's a delicate-looking Boston blonde whose middle name is tenacity.)

About five they let us try to go home. Edith went through the city and saw long lines of stretchers being carried to the hospital. I went along the river, past the airport, where things looked normal until I came to the Generalissimo's headquarters, around which everything was destroyed although the building itself was all right. The street was so full of rubble that I couldn't get past, so I plunged into a maze of small alleys trying to find a detour. Every time I thought I was getting through I met fleeing refugees and had to turn back.

I'll never forget the sight of people running from fire with whatever they could pick up: a baby and a rusty teakettle, a briefcase and a quilt, anything they could grab, and the tense, frozen stare as they entered an unknown future. Most of all I remember the many women with one baby in arms, one on the back, one begging to be taken up, and one unborn. The Bible says, "Woe to them that are with child and to them that give suck in that day."

I heard that the pavement was broken on San P'ai Fang, our street, and that there were fires near there, but I couldn't learn anything about Hsuang Hangtze, the little lane leading down from the main street to our door. At last I came out again near the Generalissimo's headquarters, and the clean-up had progressed enough so that I could pick my way through.

After wandering for an hour and a half, I reached home. There was the house as good as new! I hurried up the four flights to our place, and found Wally lying exhausted in the long chair. From the window I could see the few remaining timbers of the shacks below the city wall still blazing.

Wally had come out of his office dugout and seen fires near our house. He ran through a ghastly area and spent the afternoon packing the most important things and dragging them downstairs, and carrying things for Mrs. Wang, who was alone with her baby. The heat was terrific, and he thought the house might catch at any time. Fortunately it is one of the few solid structures in that part of town. Most of Chungking is little better than tinder. The shacks along the top of the wall were torn down to keep the fire below the wall from spreading into the city.

When it was clear that the house was safe, Wally carried everything up four floors again, thus reaching the state of exhaustion in which I found him. I've been in a daze since then because everything we own is like mince pie. He just threw things around, picking out the important things to save. All our good clothes were jammed pell-mell into suitcases, and came out a mass of wrinkles. But that's a small thing to complain about.

At bedtime we heard a great banging on kettles and drums. Chiang Sao said a dog was eating the moon, and people had to drive it away. We went to the door and saw an eclipse in progress. Knowing that the people always succeed in driving the dog away, we went to sleep.

Thursday morning I walked all the way to work (fifty minutes) as every rickshaw was carrying refugees out of town. There was a false alarm at noon. I went home before four so Chiang Sao could go to check up on her son, but she had already heard from him.

The sirens were still not working. We were to go to Frank's for dinner, but Wally thought I wasn't ready and I thought he wasn't ready, so we waited for each other for about five minutes before starting. When we had walked about fifteen minutes people began to run, and guards swarmed out and put us into a large theater building. We had just time to hide under the ticket counter before the bombs began to fall. It was soon over. We began to get the stench of incendiary bombs.

When we were allowed to go out there were already huge fires in two areas, one ahead of us and one behind. If we had left home five minutes earlier or later we would have been in the thick of it. Refugees were streaming by with whatever they could grab of their possessions. There was nothing to do but find a way home. We met a friend whose house had collapsed, but the walls being just bamboo and plaster, he pushed them off and came out. He was all powdered with plaster dust, and was on the way to the hospital where his wife was expecting a baby.

From our flat roof we could see terrific conflagrations, but we didn't watch long. We turned away to watch the moon rise over the mountains, and then went to bed. We are learning not to get gray hair over things we can't help.

There was no new damage between home and the embassy, so I was able to walk to work Friday morning. People were still pouring out of the city. The government had been trying for months to get non-essential people out, but without success. They had to be bombed before they would leave a boom town with so many chances to get rich in business, or exchange their city houses and markets for country living.

There had also been a plan to tear down houses to make fire lanes, so fires couldn't spread so, but people get awfully upset if you try to tear down their houses. Now the Japanese have created fire lanes far beyond what was planned. With every fire, the rest of the city becomes safer.

Friday there was no alarm, but also little food to be had. Farmers didn't want to come into the city. I took our last eggs and bread for my breakfast and my lunch sandwiches. We had rice on hand, and luckily some home-salted pork and some cookies, so we didn't go hungry. Even the embassy people had little but rice that day. Saturday Chiang Sao went out before six and managed to buy some lard, some pickled eggs, and some foreign cabbage and onions—things that will keep. Now she tries to keep food on hand, contrary to the usual custom of buying only for the day. We still haven't been able to get bread, but the embassy cook has been baking, and gives me some to eat with my hard eggs at noon. I scramble eggs with cooked rice for breakfast, and Chiang Sao, by going very early to market, manages to give us a fairly good supper.

Saturday we had a false alarm, and Sunday none at all. I crossed the river early to scout out ways to take care of brother Irving, whose tuberculosis now tests positive. He is still in the Canadian hospital, but must soon find another place to stay.

Every hallway of the hospital was lined with wounded lying on mats. Miss Harris, the head nurse, was looking as fresh and crisp as ever, but said she felt exhausted. Dr. Allen did abdominal surgery and amputations for forty-eight consecutive hours, and I know she was in there too.

I walked to Jim and Mary Endicott's to consult with them. Jim was out feeding refugees and arranging for the construction of a refugee camp, but I had a pleasant day with Mary and the children. She tries not to let them hear much about the disaster. The youngest boy will scarcely stir from her side since it happened.

Jim and Ch'u Djang came in, dead tired, and slept for half an hour. Then we had tea and talked about our problems, about which more later.

So another long, lovely walk through the countryside with refugees under every tree, and back across the river. Wally wasn't there, and I knew he had been feeding refugees all day and would be tired, so I took a bath while waiting for him. That sounds as if I climbed into a nice, hot tub, but of course all we can have is sponge baths. At eight he still hadn't come, so I ate alone.

At midnight Wally came in, tired to death. I was just telling him about my day when we got our first night alarm. We put on dark clothes, and took our briefcase of valuables to the basement, which we think is safer than our sketchy shelter. The alarm lasted until about half past four. Poor Wally, who had had no sleep, was wilting. I sat on a chair with my head against the wall and tried to doze. He sat on a stool with his head on the briefcase on my lap, and got such rest as he could.

No bombs were dropped. One plane kept circling over the city, perhaps just to keep us from sleeping, as they used to do in Canton. About three-thirty a.m., we went back to bed, but I kept one ear open until the clear signal.

I got to work on time Monday morning, but since most of my pupils were too bleary to take their lessons, I napped on a sofa in the club room. There have been no more alarms. I am storing a few things at the embassy in case of a fire at home.

The English paper resumed publication today. It calls the bombings of May third and fourth, last Wednesday and Thursday, the most merciless of the war, and I can believe it. They say that Japan boasted over the radio that they would wipe out Chungking between May third and ninth. That time is past now, and although the richest parts of the city are gone, I'd say Chungking has a good deal of vitality left. When will they learn that terrorism just stiffens people's spines?

We went last evening to see a member of the Legislative Yuan. He said the police have buried two thousand four hundred coffins. There is no record of the people buried privately. People I know think it barbarous to try to put them all into coffins. They should go into a common grave, as is usual in great disasters, but the Chinese feeling about being buried in a coffin is so strong that the government thinks it best to do so. A reasonable estimate of the number killed in those two days is six to eight thousand. The Japanese have never used so many incendiary bombs before, and Chungking is very flammable.

Last night on our way Wally suddenly made a turn, apparently into a pile of broken bricks. I asked, "Where are you going?"

"This is the way we always go," he replied.

I looked around and could see no landmark in any direction. What had been a wide paved street had a little footpath cleared through it.

Journal, Chungking, May 13, 1939

There have been no more raids except one yesterday, when bombs fell on the other side of the Kialing river. Our defenses have been much improved, and we brought down at least three planes. There were a few small fires, but the fire squads are more experienced now, and soon had them under control. Houses have been torn down to make fire lanes, which should have been done long before.

A relative came this morning and said he had lost everything in the fire. We gave him a little money to tide him over, pending a clan conference to decide what to do for him.

I think it is impossible for us to go to Sumatra. They sent a very attractive contract, but we must send it back. Early on May third, the day of the first bombing, a man came from Great China University in Kweiyang (a refugee school from Shanghai) to offer Wally a job teaching economics. They wanted me to teach, too. It was just the job for Wally—the courses he likes best plus research work. One of their teachers had left suddenly, and they wanted Wally at once. We immediately promised to go, and this Mr. King made arrangements for our transportation. Wally went about the formality (as he thought) of resigning. He had supposed that Colonel Huang would be glad to see him go.

To our surprise, the resignation was flatly and unpleasantly refused. There is an order from Chiang Kai-shek that no one is to leave a government or military organization for the duration of the war. They have always emphasized that New Life is neither government nor military, but Colonel Huang also heads many other organizations, and could report Wally as a military deserter. Of course we hadn't thought how bad it would look to run away just now with the press of refugee work, and the prevailing panic. I talked to Jim Endicott, who thought it was absolutely right for Wally to go to work in his own field, but he was unable to influence the colonel.

Mr. King had gone back to Kweiyang with our promise to go. We went to a member of the board of directors of the university, who is also a member of the Legislative Yuan. He wouldn't take no for an answer. He said they needed Wally and he would leave no stone unturned to get him. He talked to the colonel, and had the dean and others bombard him with letters, but to no avail.

So I'm afraid we are here to stay. Wally has been living on dreams of a new job, but he will try to make the best of it.

Chapter 13

Letter, Chungking, May 26, 1939

Dear Folks,

I've just finished correcting the strange English of a little book of avia-tors' personal experience stories translated into English by someone I'd love to meet if he talks the way he writes. It's going into a second edition, and I've been asked to correct it first, for free of course. I've done unpaid editorial work for everyone from Mme. Chiang down, and written letters for Madame. Colonel Huang gets the credit. I can't resist giving you a sample from a man whose plane was shot down: "I fell into a swampy pond and while making a languid effort to get up I was led to ponder that the danger through which I had just passed was like a dream."

But I suppose you are more interested in us than in that. We're still doing fine. We were at home during last night's bombing but there was nothing near us. Wally is talking about sending me to the hills for the sum-mer, but I'd rather find a place with a good dugout and stay with him. We are dividing our things, to store some at the embassy and some across the river, so they can't all be lost at once.

The American Embassy has set up a committee of men to whom we must report after raids, so they can check up on us quickly. Last evening before the clear signal Arnold Vaught and Arthur Allen came to check on me, to save me the trouble.

I suppose your papers have made things sound worse than they are, but actually they have been bad enough. Business hours are now six to nine, morning and evening, and most shops never take all their shutters down at all, but still the city is far from being either dead or daunted. People actually use the rubble to build themselves makeshift shelters.

My watch, the family's only timepiece, was out for repair. I've heard that the bank across from the shop was bombed, so I don't know whether I have a watch or not. Wally went early this morning to see, but he isn't back yet.

Love to all,

Letter, 7 Dai Chia Hang, Chungking, May 30, 1939

Dear Folks,

After a strenuous weekend, we are now ensconced in the Methodist Mission Ladies' House at the above address. All the ladies have fled to the hills except that Alma Erickson, the head nurse, sometimes stays down here. We have the use of an admirable cave.

The house is an immense foreign-style structure with two floors of big rooms, full basement and attic. It has a wide veranda on three sides upstairs and down. We expect to sleep out there on the second floor, where I slept last year after Katie's death. There is a great view over the river to the hills, and we can see the sunset.

We've told Chiang Sao to find a woman she can trust to stay with her, partly because it's a big place for her to take care of and partly because she's afraid to stay there alone.

Now for the events that led to the move.

Sunday Wally went in search of my watch which was being repaired when the shop was bombed. There was a notice that they had moved to the country. He found out that he can get the watch next week.

I went across the river to try to get permission to store things in some-body's house. I waited three hours in the sun on the shore to get across the river. On the other side I found another American Mrs. Liu (one of six registered at the American Embassy) and her husband and son. They were going to Kweiyang, but found that they must wait a week for a bus ticket. They shared with me the lunch they had prepared for the trip, and I suggested that they stay at the Canadian Mission so as not to have to take their things across the river again. This was lucky, as you shall see, and saved Wally a bad night.

Then, all the sedan chairs and litters being busy, and I by no means dressed to ride a pony, I set off on foot for Cool Wind Gap, where most of the foreigners have their summer bungalows. It's a stiff climb and I arrived, pant-ing and dripping, sometime after one o'clock. Eleanor McCurdy, who is a dar-ling, fell on my neck and gave me a second lunch and a breezy nap in a long chair among the tall pines.

She said that I mustn't go back that day. To cross the river before bomb-ing hours I'd have to leave at once, which was out of the question. After hours it would be too late to cross alone, even in normal times, and not to be thought of among the crowds that would be going back after taking refuge in the coun-try for the day. She thought if there was no raid, Wally wouldn't worry too much, and if there was one there would be newspaper men going down and I could go with them. With some misgivings, I stayed.

At five all the foreigners from the neighborhood and some Chinese, including Soo Mo, whom you knew at Carleton, came for a sing. When the Methodist Mission ladies heard that I wanted a house with a good dugout they asked me to move into theirs. They'd feel safer to have someone in it. One of them read me a lecture about staying in the city at all. She said, "It's your duty to leave. The only duty of a woman at a time like this is to get out of the way and not be a burden on the men."

If I had children I'd leave in a minute, but since I haven't I think any place safe enough for Wally is safe enough for me. I'd be a bigger burden if I left. Eleanor McCurdy would stay in town if she weren't responsible for running the hill bungalow and she often comes down for a few days. Mrs. Rape stays in town. Alma Erickson is here much of the time, bearing the brunt of moving and reorganizing the hospital, and she has done heroic service in many ways.

So it was arranged. I had a lovely afternoon and evening in that beautiful place with nice people to talk English with. I enjoyed the moonlight over the valley and the murmur of the pines. I was only worried lest Wally be worried about me.

Eleanor arranged for me to go down at five in the morning with Cheng K'ang-chi of the Ministry of Foreign Affairs, and Soo's husband, who works in the Central Bank. We fairly galloped down the mountains, reaching the shore before six. On the way we overtook a mail caravan from Kweiyang, about one hundred horses, heavily laden with mail sacks, struggling down the stone stairs. Once the Vaughts received a copy of Asia *that was crumpled and muddy. Someone in the P.O. had written on it in English, "So sorry, the horse fell over a cliff."*

Even so early, we had to wait nearly an hour to cross the river. Mr. Cheng had had a bad night and no breakfast. I noticed that he pressed against me, and I thought the crowd was pushing him, until he murmured, "I'm fainting." I saw that he was leaning against me like a log of wood, his face ghastly, and sweating rivers. I told him to hold on to me until it cleared. Soo's husband supported him on the other side. He opened his eyes sometimes but couldn't see anything. He asked in a frightened little voice, "What shall I do?" We feared he might slump down at any moment, but he managed to keep his feet. When the ferry came we held back the crowd with our elbows and got him to a seat, where we fanned him. By the time we got across the river he felt well enough to go home alone in a sedan chair. I asked about him later, as he is staying at McCurdy's, next door to our house, while his wife, Nien Cheng, is on a mission to England. After resting a couple of hours he went to his office.

I got home about seven and found that Wally had indeed been worried. It occurred to him that I might have gone to the Canadian Mission if I couldn't get across the river, so he went to his office and called Dr. Allen, who assured him that a Mrs. Liu was spending the night there. That made it all right.

When I told Wally about the house he wasn't enthusiastic. He still wanted to get me near the embassy. He said we'd go to look it over that evening. I told Chiang Sao to get ready to move, as we might go soon. She had been wonderful, calm and dependable, and hadn't seemed frightened at all, but when I mentioned moving her mask fell off. She cried out, "Oh, can we go today? I've been so frightened!" I told Wally if he had seen her face he wouldn't delay. We owed it to her to act.

So we both took the day off and all three worked like crazy to get us moved. By evening I was thoroughly exhausted, but happy. Of course there's a lot left to move. The high point of the day was shepherding five porters and two dogs through a mile of ruined streets, trying to keep them all in sight. Or maybe it was relaxing in a long chair on the breezy upstairs veranda and thinking of the quiet evenings to come in that lovely place, with a garden for the dogs to romp in. We'll be there all summer unless the house is bombed, and if the ladies don't come back in the fall we can stay indefinitely.

A few days later—I must get this off today. We're going to be very comfortable in the new house. We have a water carrier, a young boy related to one of the hospital workers. He will carry water and wash floors for four k'uai a month. That may not sound like much to you, but Chiang Sao first came to us for two, and up to the time when the bombing began she got only five. Last month we raised her to six and have promised her seven next time in appreciation of her fine spirit. We have given her medical care, which cost more than her wages, and she has tips from guests when we have parties, and she can sell tin cans and old papers. In her spare time she makes shoe soles to sell. She considers it a profitable position, and has nearly paid off the debts that drove her into service.

We recently learned her story. Her family was fairly well off as farmers go. When her husband died she managed the farm alone, but three years of drought drove her into debt. She knew that she was heading for disaster if she lived on borrowed money, so she got a relative to manage the farm, and she came into town to do any work she could find. She got her daughter married, and apprenticed her son to a silversmith. After having had some pretty tough jobs, she has become quite attached to us, as we have to her. She is a fine person.

Now I must mail this.

Love to all,

Chapter 14

There is not another letter home until September 10th. Whether I didn't write or whether the mail failed to get through, I don't know. I'm sure many letters were lost. I remember that summer as a long blur of coping. The food pinch didn't last long, as ways were found to bring food into the city, but even so I lost twenty pounds. It was a fifty-minute walk from the mission to the embassy. It was supposed to be twenty minutes from the first alarm to the urgent call. During the first twenty minutes of my walk I'd be able to run back to my starting point. During the last twenty I could run to my destination. That left a gap of ten minutes when I wouldn't have known where to run, so I walked as fast as I could. I never did have to use one of the public dugouts, which were dark and crowded and smelly.

Calcutta has sometimes been called the most miserably hot city in the world. Having lived in both, I award the palm to Chungking. Calcutta has a sea breeze at night, while Chungking does not. People would go out in the evening, unable to endure their homes. If a tiny current of air was detected coming up some little alley from the river, people would crowd there to feel it until their massed bodies cut it off. It must be said that, as the bombing continued and large areas were burned out, the movement of air improved.

While we lived on Hsuang Hang-tze we had any breeze there was, as we were four stories above the city wall and had windows on all sides. At the mission we were open to the river.

I remember the great variety of fruits and vegetables in the market, for many of which I still have no English name. Peaches, pears, oranges and unknown delicacies were in mouth-watering abundance, but no apples.

In July I received a fat letter for Soo Mo, sent to me in the hope that I might know where to find her. It was a round robin from her old dorm-mates at Carleton. It gave a vivid picture of the struggles of young American women coping with the Great Depression. Soo let me read it, and I said it made our problems look simple. Although I was not a member of that group, I felt moved to add a contribution, from which I will quote.

Letter, Chungking, July 7, 1939

Dear Classmates,

The accumulated Robin reached me a few days ago and I went exploring through the mountains until I found where Soo is camping. I found her bathing her baby in a one-room shack which was built for servants' quarters behind a foreigner's hill bungalow. She had made it neat and tidy, with wooden floor and mat ceiling and several coats of whitewash, and had put in an extra door and window, so it was light and airy. She was about to build a mat shed outside for her own servants.

At the moment she had no servants. She had fired her cook because he was dirty, and her amah had run away for fear of bombs. She was hoping to get new ones right away. You who keep house without servants in America may snort, but here it's a real feat, especially out in the hills away from markets and water supply. Soo's husband works in the Shanghai Bank and gets up to see her twice a week.

Soo shared your letters with me, and it was fun to read of people settling into their own little homes, with gardens to work in, and milk and butter for their children, and no question about whether it is right to have babies in such times. Some of you spoke about moving around too fast to be able to form roots, so maybe you can sense our wistfulness as we drift on the surface of life with our roots dangling, reaching for a place to strike in, but knowing nothing can really take root until the storm's over.

We went through three months of bombing in Nanking, but we never really learned what bombs can do until this spring. This city was so congested and so flammable that incendiary bombs could do appalling things the first few times. It can never be so bad again; the population has been thinned out to the capacity of the shelters, so now there are few casualties.

The ladies of the Methodist Mission ran away to the hills when it began, leaving their house empty. Wally and I moved into it as caretakers in exchange for the use of the excellent air raid shelter. The hospital has moved away except for a skeleton staff, so there is lots of room. It's comic, in a way, that we moved for safety to a place from which the ladies fled in such terror that some of them won't come back even on rainy days.

I give English lessons at the Soviet Embassy six days a week. It's interesting and very well paid. They give me both Soviet and American holidays, which is nice. I'm having a vacation now because I got too run down after a touch of malaria. Wally is in charge of the students' summer rural service work, which takes him away a good deal.

We loved seeing all your letters, even if they weren't meant for us. Would you let this circulate with the Robin by way of our greeting to the old gang?
Good wishes to all,

Letter, Chungking, September 10, 1939
Dear Folks,
    This may be my last letter from here. Wally will leave for Kweiyang in about a week, whenever he can get transportation. He still doesn't have permission to leave his job, but we're going anyway. I expect to follow at the end of the month. That will make me a few days late for classes and give me another 500 pay at the embassy, which we need for moving. Since the Soviets voluntarily doubled my pay to make up for the falling exchange, it almost seems silly for me to go at all. Each pupil pays me 100 a month, so I total from $500 to $700—fabulous money for anyone on a Chinese living standard.
    I refused to take full time work at Ta Hsia (Great China University) so I will teach only eight hours a week, and hope to have some time for writing. I don't know yet what my salary will be, but probably not much over $100 a month. That, with Wally's $240, would be enough for ourselves, but we have to support Irving, who is still incapacitated by his tuberculosis.
    It's Wally's big chance to get back to teaching, and away from the New Life Movement. We must take it even if it does mean my teaching horrible huge classes for a pittance, instead of interesting private lessons for good pay. The people we have met from Ta Hsia are very nice and cooperative.
    Kweiyang will be a very different place to live. It's a small city that used to be one of the poorest and most remote in China, but is now a bustling junction of the new trade routes. It does not have frequent air raids, although an incendiary raid last February 4th wiped out the whole center of the city. One can walk across it in a few minutes, so there won't be the hours lost over inefficient transportation that we have here. In summer it never goes over ninety degrees. There is an old saying that in Kweichow (the province where Kweiyang is) the sky is never clear for three days, the earth is never level for three feet, and no family has three ounces of silver.
    The university is outside the city wall, five minutes' walk from the beginning of the high mountains, into which we will scatter in case of air raids (surely pleasanter than sitting in a cave). There won't be all the currents of government and social activities that there are in Chungking, but there will be people passing through and waiting for transportation, and the International Relief Committee has its headquarters there. I will have an introduction to them. We can probably have our own little house near the campus.

We spent about four hours in the cave for four nights during the full moon, but the bombing was all outside the city in the new sections that people have moved out to. They haven't come except on moonlit nights for a long time because our defenses are so good.

Someone has come to invite us out to dinner, so I must change my grass mules for shoes that need resoling again, and go to a swank new Russian restaurant called the Casino.

Letter, Chungking, September 12, 1939
Dear Folks,

A package of stockings came—nine pairs! That's wealth! I shouldn't have to worry about stockings again for two years unless they get bombed, and I can store some in another place as insurance against that. The darning cotton is precious too. It's of such a color that I can fix up my old silk stockings for a few more great occasions. The typewriter ribbon is a treasure. Many, many thanks!

Letter, Chungking, September 22, 1939
Dear Folks,

There is news that airplanes are coming, but I can at least start a letter while waiting for the alarm. It's very tiresome. A week of rain and clouds while the moon approached full gave us much appreciated nights of rest. Last night, one day after full moon, the weather cleared and we had two alarms, at least two hours each. People resent losing sleep that way. It messes up your whole day. Here are the sirens already and it's only seven-thirty. They must be going to make a night of it.

I've never heard such a desperate cacophony as the Chungking alarms. First the sirens, not all on the same key, and then the boat whistles on the river with discordant shrieks, and the sound of dozens of cracked, rusty old bells and gongs, hauled from temples around the country to do duty when the power is off. Dogs and babies get nervous at the first sound (Jeannie can hear it before I can) but I just get brutally bored.

Wally has been gone for nearly two weeks, and I'm to go as soon as I can. Wally was afraid we'd have to live in a hotel, $66 for one small room. He took Jeannie with him because she was about to give birth, and he was desperate about what to do with her and her pups. Now he has found three rooms in the home of a friend of Frank's, Dr. Sheng K'e-fei, known to his friends as Coffee, head of the Central Hospital. We can board with him and won't have to have our own servant at all.

Wally says living in Kweiyang is even higher than here. Our rent will be only $20, but he had to spend $35 to have the rooms papered with white paper, and $19 for a bed like the one we got for $8 here. Our income won't be more than enough to live modestly.

If I hadn't promised to go it might make sense for me to stay here a few more months. I'd make $700 a month here, and could save more in a short time than I'll get in a year there. But it would queer Wally if I didn't go now. At least I insisted on having only part time.

I've had Chiang Sao's niece sewing for me for several days. You'd laugh at what she has made of hand-woven cotton cloth, about like flour sacking. I got a lot last year for baby things for only twenty-eight cents a foot. I'd have to pay at least seventy now for anything better, so I just used what I had.

Love to all,

Chapter 15

Journal, Kweiyang, October, 1939

I left Chungking October 8th by bus. The last seven nights there we had alarms every night, and sometimes twice a night, lasting from two to six hours each time. Of course the planes would be over the city only a few minutes, but when you share a cave with several hundred people you can't run in and out. You have to go in and stay put.

I usually went to the dugout with Arthur Allen of the YMCA and Rewi Alley of the Industrial Cooperatives, who lived next door at the McCurdy's. Mac and Eleanor McCurdy never went to the dugout because Eleanor had claustrophobia. They had a foxhole in their yard. I carried a medium-sized covered basket which I put on my lap, put my arms on it, and my head on my arms, thus getting some rest.

I got my bus ticket for Thursday and had to get my things to the China Travel Service the day before. It cost $106 for the things that would cost more to replace than to ship. We had thought we didn't have much, but it turned out to be a pile.

Thursday morning there was an alarm, the first in daytime for a long time, but it was over in time for me to take the ferry across the river for my one o'clock bus, which would leave from Hai T'an Hsi on the other bank. On the way I met Mr. Lu, whom I had met at Frank's house. He took care of me the whole way, giving me the window seat, and running to find me a good room at each stop. This was lucky for me, as I'm still a bit of a greenhorn.

There was another foreigner on the bus, a Mr. Myer, a missionary going for his first home leave. I was interested to see that, after five years in China, he still had his Sunday School concept of the "heathen Chinese." Amazing how people can go through life seeing only what they expect to see.

It rained a good part of Thursday, and the road was buttery, but the driver was very competent. We reached Kikiang on schedule the first night. I had a very plain, very clean room to myself at a hotel for $1.80.

Friday the weather was fine. A peasant lost his head and dashed in front of the bus and was thrown several feet. We stopped while his friend examined him and said he wasn't dead. We drove on, but I think he must have *needed help he didn't get. Mr. Myer said, "How can he know right away whether he's dead?"*

At one we stopped at a sizable town so the driver could repair the bus. We ate part of a lunch before the bus began honking to collect its chicks. A little after three the driver and mechanic got out and fussed around under the bus. The crankcase was leaking oil, and we had only two quarts left to take us thirty miles. At last they decided to go ahead, at the risk of burning out the bearings. We drove on up the hardest part of a notorious stretch of serpentine road. After an hour, more than a mile from the top of the pass, we stopped. The gas line was plugged. We had a mechanic but no tools, not even a wrench or screwdriver. Another car was being repaired near by, so we borrowed what we needed. When they were ready to go they took everything back, leaving our job half done. Our driver sent a message to T'ung-tze to have help sent back.

After six, when it was already nearly dark, we all decided to walk to the top of the pass where there was an open air eating place next to a police station. There was a woman with a baby less than a month old, but she was a good sport. We all made ourselves comfortable in the crude, open shelter, which had several bamboo long chairs. We exhausted the supply of noodles and made inroads on the rice. A major-general invited me to share a delicious dish of pig liver with tomatoes.

About nine we saw our rescue car coming out from town. Mr. Lu and Mr. Myer got into a discussion about whether a person could be a Christian and still smoke and drink moderately. It was fortunately terminated by the arrival of the bus. We drove on, followed by the rescue car.

At five minutes past ten we came to the city gate of T'ung-tze. It was closed tight. We honked. No answer. We kept on honking and got a sleepy reply that the gate could not be opened after ten o'clock. We protested that there were babies in the bus, and we had to get into town. After some telephoning to confirm that a bus was overdue, half a dozen soldiers, fully armed, came out to look us over. Finding us harmless, they opened the gate wide and let us in. They weren't going to let the rescue car in too, but the driver told them not to be stuffed shirts (t'sao pao, or grass package) and they gave in.

The China Travel Service hotel was full, but there was another nearby. My bed, like that of the night before, was hard boards with only one layer of quilt by way of mattress, but it was clean, and I slept well.

Saturday morning I met the others outside before seven, as usual. There was no bus. About eight it appeared, but it was going back to Chungking. We were to wait for another one, which came about ten. It was better looking than the other, but its valves needed grinding and it had no pull. The driver, also, was no good. We loafed along. At noon we stopped at Tsun-yi, where we should have been the night before. At five-twenty we got to a village called Hsi-feng, less than three hours' drive from Kweiyang, and the driver said we would spend the night there.

Old hands who knew the road said this was the worst place to stay. They urged him to go on, but he wouldn't discuss it. He said it would be crazy to drive this rotten bus after dark. Mr. Lu dashed to see what kind of room he could find me. It was a board cubicle about seven by eight feet, lined with dirty white paper, and with no window. The bed was covered with a thick straw mat. Most of the remaining space was occupied by a rough board table with a vegetable oil lamp on it, just a saucer with a bit of pith draped over the edge. They brought me a quilt, which fortunately I couldn't see well in the dim light. I climbed up on the bed and tore the paper from a little barred space under the roof to get some air. I sprinkled pyrethrum powder liberally everywhere.

I asked the boy for a ma tung. *Evidently the word didn't fit his dialect. He asked the woman with the tiny baby, who was struggling to get organized in the next room. She didn't know what it was either, but her husband explained that it was a chamber pot. The boy brought an old wooden tub about a foot across. "Will this do?" "Nicely," I replied.*

I offered my bug powder to the family, (man, woman and three children in a two-bed room) and they were charmed with it. They hadn't known about it before, and resolved to invest heavily in it if it could be had in Kweiyang.

After consuming a bowl of noodles with eggs in it, I added more bug powder to the bed and lay down with my brief case for a pillow, the dirty quilt around my lower part, and my coat over my shoulders. I wasn't conscious of any visitors, although later I found two tiny blood spots on the lining of my coat. Wally wouldn't have been able to sleep a wink in that place. The very thought of a bedbug upsets him.

The room cost eighty cents. I added ten cents for the paper I tore, and thirty for the old tub, though they said they hadn't the face to charge for so poor a thing.

Sunday we started about seven and got to Kweiyang at ten. Wally had waited late for me the night before, but hadn't supposed we'd come so early in the morning. Mr. Lu took me to the house at 65 Fu Teh Kai (Wealth and Morality Street). The things I had shipped were on the same bus, so we brought them along.

Jeannie came prancing to meet me, having delivered herself of six pups two days before.

On the way to the house I passed through the area that was burned out by incendiary bombs. There were new buildings all along the street, but peering behind them you could see a vast, devastated area. Kweiyang is such a small city that it can be evacuated in a few minutes, so there is little danger to life, but only to things. After the big fire they tore down the city wall except for the gates, so people could get out easily and not be trampled at the gate as they had been that time.

Letter, c/o College of Commerce, Great China University, Kweiyang, Kweichow, China, October 18, 1939
Dear Folks,

We are sharing a house with China's leading surgeon, Sheng K'e-fei (Coffee), head of the Central Hospital, which has branches here and in Chungking. We have three rooms on the south side of the court. It's the first time I've lived in a purely Chinese house. The only foreign things about this house are the electric lights and the padlocks. The padlock hasps are of hand-wrought iron, the hinges are wood, and the windows are latticework with paper pasted over it. They are hung with wooden hinges at the top, and may be propped open with a stick.

Wally spent $34 to have two rooms papered with white paper, more than twice what it would have cost a year ago. The bedroom has a wooden floor, the other two rooms a floor of packed earth mixed with lime. The middle one, which will be our living room, has no furniture yet. It is freshly covered with finely-woven straw mats, laid over a sprinkling of lime to keep them from rotting. The third room has been left as it was. It is Jeannie's room for now, with a pile of straw for the pups and a paper spread under her bowl. I find the place quite pleasant.

Contrary to the saying that the sky is never clear for three days, it has been beautiful every day since I came, eleven days ago. Tuesday, Wednesday and Thursday there were alarms, as if to welcome me. It gave us good fire drill ex-perience. We know now where to go, and how long it will take to get there. Of course the planes weren't coming here at all. Kweiyang has been bombed only twice. We sat for some time on a mountainside, enjoying the autumn sunshine. It's lots more fun than a dugout, and just as safe. There are never night alarms here. They come like gentlemen at midday. I think I'll like it here.

As Tuesday was the Double Tenth (October 10, anniversary of the founding of the Republic), I didn't start teaching until Wednesday. I have more than I wanted. I had set nine hours a week as the most that I was willing to do, and they had promised me four hours each of sophomore

English and beginning French. I found that they had also assigned me three hours of English conversation, than which there is nothing harder to teach so that it is worth anything. That gives me eleven hours at $3 an hour, with nothing for vacations or days off. One more hour would make me full time with twelve-month pay. It leaves me holding the bag. I had definitely refused full time. I don't want to queer Wally by making a big fuss. I'll survive, but I don't like it. There goes the time I had hoped to have for writing.

We have breakfast and supper with the hospital people. Their servant, Lao Hsia, is very good, but without Chiang Sao's strength and initiative. He cleans our floors and buys the materials for our lunch. I do the room work and washing myself (laundry costs twenty cents per piece here). Every morning I go to the kitchen to prepare Jeannie's food: a bounteous cauldron of rich stew made from pork bone (free), chopped beef, cabbage leaves and some rice. It's better food than many a man gets. I wouldn't mind eating it myself except that I'd add some salt and seasonings. When Lao Hsia fed her he mixed hunks of raw beef with left-over rice, and gave her the bones (if any) raw. She didn't like it, didn't get enough liquid, and hadn't enough milk for the pups. Now with the same materials, plus the coarse leaves of the cabbage, she and the pups are flourishing. The puppies are the progeny of a fine Scottie that we borrowed from someone in the diplomatic corps in Chunking. Many of our colleagues are eager to have one, but we'll keep one for ourselves. We'll call him Bobby, and he will be company for Jeannie since Jackie left with Ruth Hemenway.

We cook our own lunch, the same every day: three bowls of noodles cooked with pig liver, greens, and tiny tomatoes the size of cherries. It's a very nourishing and palatable dish. I already feel that I'm putting back some of my lost twenty pounds.

The only "fruit" available at this season, is ti lo pu (earth turnip). [Ed. note, 1992—This is now available in America as jicama.] It is a root vegetable which is sweet and crisp, tender and juicy when small, and can be eaten raw. They are very good and also cheap.

Classes start at seven-thirty and end late in the afternoon, leaving the middle of the day free for alarms. They are shortened to forty-five minutes, with five-minute intervals. Monday I have no classes. Tuesday and Thursday I stay an extra hour for Chinese lessons with one of my French pupils, a general's daughter named Ma Shih-fang.

I've decided not to have a servant, but to spend what one would cost on making the place easier to work in. We haven't enough work to keep anyone busy.

Every day I get up when Wally does, have breakfast with him, wash clothes in what's left of the hot water Lao Hsia brings us, and put the place in order. If I leave anything undone, Lao Hsia will do it when he comes to do the floors, but he's not supposed to be our servant, and I don't like to have someone else tidy up and put things where I can't find them. I am forced to be tidy in self-defense.

The attempt to do everything keeps me more alert than I've been for a long time. I can feel my fitness improving over when I sat around the embassy all day and the air raid shelter all night. Our income here will be slim, but we feel more alive.

My classes are satisfactory as classes go. No magic has made me love teaching classes, but I can make a job of it. I have several auditors, and the doorway of the classroom is usually full of people listening, but that's because I'm a curiosity rather than because of any peculiar charm in my lessons. Not only am I the first foreign teacher in this student generation, but the president created notoriety for me before I came by announcing that I was giving up a job worth nearly a thousand a month to come here. Naturally everyone wants to take a squint at the crazy mug who would do that.

I'm planning on creating some notoriety for myself next week. There will be hill climbing races, one for the men faculty members and one for the women. I see people out training for it, but I don't need to train, being fresh from Chungking where most of the walking is up and down stairs.

There are Miao tribespeople around here. The women's costumes are very picturesque, with dark blue accordion-pleated kilts and exquisitely cross-stitched jackets.

Tomorrow we go to the country to see the site for the new buildings that have been promised for the university. When they are built it will be a national instead of a private university. Now it is a refugee school from Shanghai, trying to manage in a run-down old temple. I've heard that the new place is very beautiful, a famous scenic spot called Hua-ch'i (Flowery River).

Love to all,

Chapter 16

I did win the hill climbing race by a wide margin.

Life was relatively peaceful for the next few months. I regained most of my lost weight, and felt more energetic. One of my pleasantest memories of the war years is of gathering with our very congenial housemates late every afternoon to eat fruit and chat until dinner was ready.

Gradually I began to show signs of stress. I had bouts of low-grade fever and general exhaustion, with no apparent reason.

One day Wally said, "Tai Li wants to send you some pupils. The person who told me said to act surprised when it happens, as he wasn't supposed to tell me."

We discussed how to handle such a request if it came. I didn't like the idea of having anything to do with the dreaded secret police, but was it safe to refuse? It was not considered healthy to cross the path of Tai Li, the shadowy, almost mythical figure who pulled the strings of the huge, repressive organizaton that spied on everyone and was blamed for numerous disappearances. My own favorite student was imprisoned for "impurity of thought" after an unusually free discussion in my classroom.

Time passed and nothing happened. Maybe it never would.

A few quotations from my journal may give some picture of how we lived.

Journal, Kweiyang, December 18, 1939

Thursday I got up and worked at my desk all morning. I met my classes in the afternoon, but got so dizzy walking over that I had to rest five minutes before the conversation class, and I just came home and rested after French. That evening Wally wanted me to read a chapter of Business Administration for him. Thinking he needed it the next day, I ploughed through it, only to find that it was for some time in the future. Meantime I had not prepared my sophomore English, so I had to get up and give it a lick and a promise Friday morning. I hate teaching by licks and promises. No matter how well you know your stuff, an unplanned lesson is a killjoy flop.

Journal, Kweiyang, December 26, 1939

*My students undertook to organize a Christmas party. You might won-
der why Christmas would be celebrated in a non-Christian country, but
Madame Chiang Kai-shek is the daughter of a Methodist preacher, and her
husband gets a lot of favorable publicity in the foreign press because of his
vaunted conversion to Christianity and his claim that he reads the Bible every
day. I have heard Methodist missionaries thanking God for "our great Christian leaders."*

*I met with the party committee, and thought they seemed well orga-
nized. I gave them $20 toward expenses. They'll get the rest from ticket sales.
The party will be at the Student Center, an interesting place with social
rooms, library, and work rooms for student self-help projects such as printing,
toy making, bookbinding, sewing and knitting. The assembly hall is fresh and
attractive, with screens and a little stage and ping-pong tables.*

*I went one day to help with the decorations, making paper chains and
cutting pine trees from green paper to pin on the curtains. On Christmas Eve
I went home after class for a nap, then went to the Center to help with final
details. I met two committee members coming out. They said there was
another meeting in the hall, taking advantage of our nice decorations, and it
wouldn't be out until six. I went home for an early supper and came back, but
the gate I knew was locked and it took me twenty minutes to find the front
entrance on another street.*

*When I got in the guests were arriving, and the committee were rushing
around trying to do in ten minutes what should have taken an hour. A special guest was Paul Moritz, a representative of a lot of student organizations,
who was spending a year in China to observe Chinese student life. I was
curious to see what the program would be, as there had been too many alarms
that week for me to keep track of what they were doing.*

*It turned out to be a typical Chinese party, with everyone sitting in a
semicircle, and a lot of musical numbers and jokes planned, and people being
dragged out of the crowd to sing or do skits. I had to lead a group singing
Christmas carols, and they also made me sing "Old MacDonald Had a
Farm" and some French nursery songs. A funny Santa Claus appeared, thin
and quavery-voiced, and apologetic about not speaking Chinese very well because he hadn't come to China very often. He gave each person a little enve-
lope with half a package of Lifesavers-type candy and a slip telling his for-
tune. Everyone was supposed to read his own, but they were too embarrassed.
I had to read them all.*

The fortunes showed a big change in student mores compared to fifteen years ago, when a girl would have had a bitter fight to be allowed to go to a school function with her own brother. Samples: "You love the girl who don't love you." "Everybody loves you." "You will engage with a rough boy." "You will get a warning from your school this term." "You will marry a man you don't like" "The girls don't like you." etc. etc.

After the program there were games with the benches all in a circle. One was called "Recover our lost territories." Each person took the name of a city in the occupied area. The leader would say, for example, "Do you want to recover Shanghai and Kalgan?" Those two cities would stand up, and the people on each side of them would have to exchange places. The leader would try to get one of the places. The one who failed to get a place would become the leader.

After that they played another game, and then they had to break up in order to be in their dormitories by ten. I proposed a vote of thanks to the committee, and a boy with a fine voice led the school song, and it was over.

I had no chance to ask Paul Moritz how it impressed him. It seemed to me suitable for grade-school children.

∾

Mary Endicott wrote to assure me of their help if Wally should get in trouble over leaving New Life, and to offer me hospitality if I should have to return to Chungking "for any reason." I appreciated her writing, but couldn't believe there would be any trouble. It was too ridiculous.

∾

Journal, Kweiyang, December 27, 1939

I have been thinking that it's silly, when I hate teaching classes of people so poorly prepared that I can never do anything but play catch up, to fill my time with teaching to the exclusion of everything else. From the standpoint of the future, it would make much more sense to try my hand at writing for publication in America this year, while my material on China is still timely enough to help me over the hurdle of first acceptance. It's impossible to write with my present schedule, so I talked to Wally about cutting down. Instead of taking on another course of composition, so as to have full time, I should ask Dean Wu to relieve me of the conversation class, which is a waste of everyone's time. We haven't come to an agreement yet, but it is clear to me: If I allow all my time to be filled with teaching, it will be so all my life, and if that's not what I want to do it's wrong to drift into a lifetime of it.

This is the best year there will ever be to try to break into writing, which is what I have always wanted to do. Just how I can do it without offending Wally's sense of expediency too much, I don't know, but somehow it must be. We're making enough between us so that I can afford to teach part time, and who knows when that will be true again? If I can sell even one little article in America it will far more than make up the difference. Isn't the gamble worth while? It seems that to Wally a small salary in hand is worth any number of stories in the bush.

He just doesn't believe I can do anything with writing, but I know I can. I'm a good writer. I just don't know how to go about marketing it from here, but I'm sure that can be solved.

Journal, Kweiyang, Monday, December 29, 1939

All day Wally and I had a terrible time trying to come to an agreement about what I should do next semester. He was adamant that I should teach full time, but he couldn't come up with a convincing reason. I was equally determined not to do so unless he had better reasons than he told me. At last I decided to do it, not because of any reason he gave, but because I felt I had let myself in for it by being too weak-kneed and wishy-washy to say no clearly in the first place, weeks ago when the plans were being made. I asserted myself only against teaching a literature course. I felt heavy-hearted about it all the time, but didn't do anything, and my silence gave consent. When the noose tightens around the neck, it's too late to avoid going to the gallows. In the future I must assert myself at the proper time.

In the end we came to a very good understanding. He promised that after this next semester he will never ask me to teach full time, and never try to arrange my work for me, but I shall make my own plans according to my own ideas. I ought to get that from him in writing, but all hell would break loose if I tried. He's against anything legalistic in personal relations.

Later—I had my two-hour French class today for once. It was a bit ragged. We've missed too many classes because of alarms. Spent the evening correcting papers. To bed early. Have felt very tired all day. Next term's schedule is weighing on me.

Chapter 17

It must have been in December that a woman I had met socially came to see me. After the usual courtesies she said, "Four girls from Madame Chiang's school for the orphans of revolutionary martyrs are to be sent to America to study. Madame wants them to improve their English and learn foreign manners before they go. Your home would be the best place for them. Of course you have no room for them here, but you would share a good house in the country with them, and be well paid for teaching them. Please consider the offer carefully. It is an opportunity to help these girls who deserve so much from us."

As I tried to formulate a non-committal reply, Wally came to the rescue. "It is an honor to be chosen for this work," he said, "but we must know more before we decide. We are under contract to the university. We must know the details of this arrangement and think whether it is compatible with our duties."

She turned to me. "How do you feel about it? These are charming girls. They would love and admire you, and you would enjoy them."

"I agree with my husband that we must know much more before we decide. Even now I am often tired, and don't know whether I could handle a second job."

"Of course your life would be much easier in a proper house with servants. It is extremely difficult to find a house outside the city. This might be your only chance."

Wally to the rescue again, "Are you authorized to explain all the details, or is there someone else we should talk to?"

"You will have to talk with the police commissioner, who will be responsible for the girls while they are here. I can set up an appointment with him for you."

After some chit-chat she left. We stared at each other.

"How do you feel about it?" asked Wally at last.

"My first reaction was shock at the idea of taking on such a job, but a house outside the city is tempting. Also it would make a perfect excuse not to take Tai Li's men if they should show up."

"That's a good point. Let's talk to the commissioner and then think it over."

So after due deliberation it was decided. Even the government was having difficulty finding a house outside the city, but in the meantime the girls would come to get acquainted and start their lessons.

The first thing they wanted was for me to give them English names. The small, vivacious one became Betty, the tall, reserved one was Julia, the athletic one was Mary, and the quiet, slow-moving one was Helen.

Their English was very poor. They would have a long way to go to be fit to study abroad, but I thought if they had been chosen for such a privilege they must be excellent students. I told them they must speak only English with me except when they had to be sure I understood something. I laid out a schedule for lessons, some as a group and some one-on-one.

They chatted in Chinese for a while, and Wally asked them about their background. They spoke of the strict discipline under which they lived. They must write a journal every day, and always wash their feet with hot water at bedtime. They had a regular schedule for everything. "Uncle Yen," the police commissioner, supervised them closely.

When they were gone, Wally voiced his suspicions. "It seems to me their stories don't fit together. We were told they were orphans of revolutionary martyrs. As such they would have been in Madame's school since they were very young, and would have little memory of any other life, but Mary said her father was killed at the battle of T'ai-erh-ch'uang and that she used to live in Shantung. Betty said she lived in Shanghai before the war. There's something fishy."

A suspicion was growing in my mind. "Do you suppose they could be Tai Li's candidates?

"I'm wondering," said Wally. "I'll be careful not to show any suspicion, but I'm surely going to keep my eyes open."

A few days later Betty was writing her journal while I gave Mary her lesson. She came to me and asked, "Who was the man who came here at two o'clock?"

Before I could answer, Wally said, "We are your teachers, and as such we have a certain relationship to you, but we also have a life of our own which does not concern you. You don't need to know who comes to our house."

Bea and Wally with pupils Julia and
Mary and Scotties Jeannie, Bobby
and Georgie, circa 1940.

Betty didn't press the point. It was clear to us that part of their training was to record everyone and everything they saw each day—a fitting discipline for spies or secret agents.

About this time, after an increasing lack of my usual drive, I developed a high fever and very sore mouth, and was in the hospital for several days. I was dismissed at last with a diagnosis of "fever of unknown origin" and referral to a dentist. The dentist found pus pockets in my gums that could explain the trouble. I had to add a twenty-minute walk to his office to my daily routine. He had a foot-pedal drill with a girl to pump it, but he made up in skill what he lacked in equipment.

He told me he had gone with an anthropological expedition to Tibet, and had never found a case of tooth decay in a Tibetan. He might have to dig through a lot of meat fibers to find the tooth, but when he found it, it was sound. He attributed this to the total lack of refined carbohydrates in the diet.

With his aggressive treatment over a period of weeks, I gradually came to feel like myself again. The treatment was in phases: (1) reduce the inflammation, (2) correct my occlusion, and (3) treat the gums surgically. He also removed my badly-placed wisdom teeth. I doubt if I could have had better care anywhere.

What we came to call "the organization" found a good house for us, but not outside the city. We had the whole upstairs of a house which qualified as "foreign style" because it had glass casement windows. We reached it by an outside stairway leading to a veranda which surrounded the house on three sides. The kitchen and a place for the male cook were at the back of the yard. We had three very large rooms which we could divide as we pleased. We had electricity and even a telephone. We had to hire an *amah* to do the general housework. A bridge from the veranda led to the *amah*'s quarters and an outhouse which, because it was so high above the pit, was free of flies or odor. Altogether it was a very high-class arrangement. There was a walled garden where we were allowed to fence a space for the dogs and one for the chickens that Wally always wanted to have.

Downstairs was a fine family headed by an old Confucian scholar who had passed the highest imperial examinations in the old days. I saw him as a dignified but rather irascible old gentleman. When he died I had a ringside seat at the very elaborate traditional funeral, with several days of ceremonies and feasting.

We got along well in the house. The girls worked hard on their English. Mary and Julia did well, but Betty and Helen showed little aptitude. Coming from a grammar-free language, they couldn't see the use of making sentences with verb forms to show time and prepositions to show relationships. If they could convey the meaning by saying, "Yesterday I go store buy shoe," why should they say, "I went to the store and bought some shoes"? Their spoken English did not improve, and their written work was worse. Julia was beginning to speak nicely while the others were still struggling.

One day there was an alarm when I was at home. Usually it came when I was at school, and I walked right out to the mountains. This time the girls offered to take me with them.

A car, unheard-of luxury for any but the very rich or influential, came to the end of our alley and we all squeezed in. They drove to a large, open space where several cars and trucks gathered. If there were an urgent alarm they would all head for their hiding places in the country, but if not they would not waste precious fuel on unnecessary driving. People gathered in groups, many smoking expensive American cigarettes.

I sat still, feeling out of place. I had a book and some paper, and spent the time making up lesson materials. Teaching without textbooks required unremitting preparation. After three quarters of an hour the clear signal sounded and we went home.

"It was like a different world," I said to Wally that night. "All those motor vehicles, and most of them burn gasoline! I saw only a few that had been converted to burn charcoal."

"What about the people? Did they look like the elite?"

"Not most of them. There were a few snazzy officer types, but most of them were rather scruffy looking. The girls seemed very much at home in the group, and knew a lot of them."

Journal, Kweiyang, Thursday, December 28, 1939

Yesterday morning I had sophomore English and came back to try to plan a story. I must try to steal a little time from my work to write a little, if I have given up hope of ever being able to sit down properly to it. I was putting it off because I always thought there'd be time next month or next year, but now I know that won't happen.

After lunch the weather had cleared, so I took the puppies out in the sunshine to play. Then I thought I shouldn't miss the chance to give Jeannie a bath on such a warm day. It's bitter cold now except when the sun shines. I had water heated, and finished just in time for the girls' lessons at three.

After that I began typing French lessons. I not only make up my textbook from day to day, but make carbons for the class of eight because the stencils they make at the school office are illegible and full of mistakes. After supper Wally needed the typewriter, so I corrected papers, made some plans and went to bed. I can finish typing this morning after the girls are gone.

It's a nuisance not to have electricity when we get up in the morning. We have it only from dusk to midnight. Every morning we have to study by candle light (candles $2.10 for six). We remind ourselves that a generation ago not even kings had electricity, but it's one thing not to miss something that doesn't exist, and another to know that it's right there, needing only to turn a switch.

Journal, Kweiyang, January 9, 1940

I had three hours of classes this afternoon, one conversation and two French. There will be only two more conversation classes ever. Whoops! Next semester I'm to have three hours of advanced English prose instead, with only a few students, and one hour of English composition to make full time. I'll get very little pay this month. Not having sick leave for part-time work almost converts me to the idea of full time.

I came home dog-tired, and had to go to the kitchen for a while, but by supper time I was dead asleep. After supper I read three Hankow Heralds *that had just come. The news of the world is more and more incredible. It seems as if European civilization is bound and determined to destroy itself. I told the kids one day how the torch of civilization has been passed from hand to hand: Egyptians to Greeks, to Romans, to Moors, to Europeans, and I said if they are no longer fit to bear it, maybe Chinese would be next.*

The journals for the next many weeks depict a stressful life with gradual recovery of my health as the periodontal disease was brought under control, lots of hiking experience as we explored places to hide from air raids in the mountains, and ceaseless effort to make sense of teaching without suitable books. A few stories are worth telling.

Christmas was a meager festival for us. Wally gave me a precious package of carbon paper he had found somehow, and I meticulously mended his favorite sweater which he had discarded as unwearable.

The girls all received identical gifts from their organization: an Omega watch, a Parker 51 pen, a pair of warm English woolen gloves with scarf to match, a Shetland sweater, a fine loose-leaf notebook, and a large box of sweets and pastries.

They had gifts for us, too, a mechanical pencil for Wally and a silk scarf for me.

"The cost of those presents would keep you and me for half a year," said Wally, "and those girls are not big shots. They are very small cogs in a big machine."

One day when I went home I found that my *amah*, Li Sao, was gone. The girls, suspecting her of stealing money and a watch, had left a marked bill lying around. When it disappeared they found it on her, and had her put in jail.

I felt sick at the thought of Li Sao and her year-old baby in prison, and I was not in a condition to get along without help. I had to get another *amah* fast. After rejecting many dirty, clumsy or incompetent applicants, I chose Ing Mei, a young girl from a Miao tribal village in the hills, who wanted to experience city life before her marriage and earn money for her trousseau. She was clean and quick and attractive in her tribal costume of pleated blue hemp cloth skirt and gaily embroidered jacket. When she had free time she was always doing wonderful, bright-colored cross stitch work on materials that would make her bridal and festival clothing. She said her father was rich. He owned five buffalo. Her mother was very clever, and did everything well.

When Wally asked her if she could read, her laughter was contagious. "What would I read a book for?"

I enjoyed teaching her our ways, and learning from her something about another way of life, but it was only for a short time. The date for her wedding was soon set, and she had to leave us. She was followed by a series of more or less satisfactory helpers.

But to get back to Li Sao, after several days I went to the prison and asked to see her. The man in charge said it was impossible. He wouldn't even go back there himself. It was too dirty and dangerous. I demanded that she be brought out to see me. After a little money changed hands she was led out by two burly guards. When she saw me she began to cry.

"I thought they were taking me out to be killed."

"What is it like where they keep you?"

"Not good. Fifteen women and children in one cell. No room to lie down. Two bowls of dirty thin rice a day. No vegetables. Some have died."

"Tell me more," I said. "I want to know all about it."

"One who had money was taken to another place. One has food sent every day by her family, but others grab it from her. Most of us have come from other places and have no one here to send us food. In the cell, the strong ones get the best places. I have to be next to the urine bucket. Sometimes it runs over. I can't live long this way. I only hope the baby dies before I do."

I gave her some sesame cakes and said I would try to help.

The guard took her back, and I returned to the man at the desk.

"How much would it cost to have her in a better place?"

"For two dollars a day she could be in a cell for six."

"What about food? She and the baby are starving."

"For another dollar she can have gruel three times a day, and some vegetables."

I pulled out fifteen dollars that I had been saving, and said, "This will be for five days. See that she is clean and well fed, and has sulphur ointment for her scabies. I will come back to see how she is."

At home I described Li Sao's condition to the girls, saying that no theft could deserve such punishment. Was there nothing they could do about it?

Mary said, "If we withdraw the complaint she will be freed."

"Why don't you do it?"

"Not unless she returns my watch," said Helen. "Criminals must not go unpunished."

My Chinese was not eloquent enough for the occasion. I asked Wally to talk to them about punishment in proportion to crime. Helen still wanted her watch back.

"Would you, personally, kill her for a watch? If she dies in prison you will have killed her, just as much as if you had done it with your own hands. Would you do that?"

She said she would think it over. When I came home the next day she had called the prison, and Li Sao had been freed.

"What can she do" I asked. "She is too sick and dirty to get work. She will have to beg."

"That's not our business," said Helen. "She can find her own way like anyone else."

Although I looked closely at every beggar woman I saw, I never found Li Sao.

When spring came the girls were taken away. Mr. Yen said they had not shown enough aptitude to be sent to America. It seemed at first we would have to move, but in the end we were allowed to take over the house, which led to another story.

A few weeks later I saw a copy of *Time* magazine which had reached the mission. It told how the Chinese government had planned to send large numbers of students to America. When the State Department found out that they were to be under surveillance while in the country, it refused them admission.

Our girls would have been the surveillance.

Chapter 18

The next journal entry, surprisingly, was written in Kikiang on the way to Chungking on February 5, 1940.

What a week it has been! One day one of the puppies fell into the toilet, down a fifteen-foot cement shaft, and came out at the bottom in such a state that we had to follow her around the yard throwing water on her before she was fit to put in a tub, and then give her six baths.

When we got home from a movie Wednesday night we found that Vice-President Ou Yuan-huai had been over and wanted Wally to get in touch with him at once on "important business." Also a note from the university asking for my overdue grades.

I sat up most of the night finishing the grades so Wally could take them over early in the morning. When he came back he said the police had been at Ta Hsia with a military warrant for his arrest on a charge of desertion of duty. Evidently Colonel Huang was making good on his promise to make trouble for him if he left New Life. The colonel also heads several military organizations.

What to do? We went to see President and Mrs. Wang. They said we must manage to put the facts before the Generalissimo or Madame Chiang. Pao Chang-ling and Wang Ju-chan suggested that Wally stay in their house until it was settled, as the police wouldn't dare take him from there. Mr. Yang (the man currently in charge of our girls) went to the police chief and got him to postpone execution of the warrant until I could go to Chungking. Wally, meanwhile, was not to try to leave town.

We wrote letters, Wally to friends who might help, and I to the Gimo and Madame, though Wally thought it best not to send those except as a last resort. Friday I went to the dentist, took the girls to an oculist, and asked Gertrude Pao to help me get a bus ticket. Saturday I wrote letters and washed woolens and served as water carrier and hanger-upper to Wally as he did the tremendous washing that we had saved up since the old house.

We worked until two a.m. Saturday night, finishing letters and packing, and got up at six so I could catch my bus.

The trip has been easy so far, and the weather not bad. Last night I slept at the new guest house (Chiao T'ai Sou) at Tung-tze. It is a really *foreign-style place with English-speaking servants from Nanking hotels. Very comfortable. Supper and room were $2.60, and breakfast twenty-five cents.*

Tonight at Kikiang I couldn't get a room at the China Travel Service, so I'm sharing a room at a new hotel with a woman who has an awfully nice baby. Tomorrow begins the campaign.

Journal, Chungking, Wednesday, February 7, 1940

The bus reached Hai T'an Hsi (across the river from Chungking) at eleven-thirty yesterday morning, making a very good trip. My suitcase was to have come on the same bus, but it didn't. I'll have to send over for it today or tomorrow. Meantime I have to wear my old green padded gown with the burned front.

The person who examined my passport said it lacked a necessary visa. He searched my suitcase, but was satisfied when the first paper he picked up was the testimonial from the university concerning Wally's and my work there.

When I got across the river I went first to McCurdy's to ask Cheng K'ang-chi to fix up my passport. I wanted my own affairs, at least, to be in order. On the way I met Phoebe taking the children to the dentist, so I knew there was no hurry about getting to her place.

I stayed at Mac's for lunch. It was International Women's Day and Eleanor was all dressed up for the meeting. Mr. and Mrs. Jimmy Yen (of the famous literacy program) were there, as he was to speak at the meeting. Knowing Mary Endicott would be there, I decided to go too and ask her where to look for Jim. Eleanor had to go early, and asked me to walk down with the Yens to show them the way.

I found Mary at once, and she told me how to call Jim. I phoned from the club, but got Ch'u Djang instead, who said he had written to Wally to try to settle it at that end. He would try to get Jim Endicott to come with him to see me that evening.

As there seemed to be nothing for me to do just then, I stayed for the meeting and met a lot of people, including Helen Chang, who used to teach with Edith and me at the embassy. She invited me to have lunch with her and Edith at the embassy today. Ruth Phillips was there and invited me to visit her up in the hills. There was also Mrs. Twinem, the one who gave up her American citizenship to serve Madame Chiang. She may possibly be useful.

I dashed back to Mac's to get my things, and then to Phoebe's, where she was expectng guests for dinner. It was a nice party.

About ten o'clock Ch'u Djang came in and we discussed what to do first. Jim thinks it is better to let Ch'u Djang handle Wally's business because he knows the Chinese ways of doing things better, and can do more spade work without attracting attention and making a big issue of it. We decided we didn't know enough to act intelligently. We must first find out what office issued the order, what person was responsible for carrying it out, what legal procedure is involved, and why the order is not being carried out in Chungking. Chu said the police and gendarme chiefs and the mayor are his friends, and he can talk to them informally without even mentioning Wally's name. Meantime Phoebe should take me to see General Chang Tze-chung, chief of Chiang's headquarters, tell him about the case, and ask him whom to approach. He is a good friend of Frank's and Phoebe's.

This morning I got up early and spent an hour putting my thoughts and my papers in order, and then went back to bed and slept until time to go with Phoebe to catch General Chang on his lunch hour.

We went to his house, a big, modern one, and talked first with his wife, an old-fashioned woman with a broad, flat, homely face and a good, motherly heart. She thought our story worthy of the general's attention, and went to put it before him. He was busy, so she came back with her daughter to talk to us until he would be free. Her eldest daughter, just back from England, is just like her in features, but as different in expression as new China is from old. Her hair is arranged with a becoming wave which makes her face, too strong for prettiness, seem less plain. In place of her mother's studied placidity, she has a forceful directness of look and manner.

To the mother Phoebe spoke of how Wally and I wanted to live together and have children, but to the daughter she spoke of common sense and basic human rights and the legal aspects of the case. I was especially impressed with the expressiveness of the girl's eyes, in contrast to the acquired flatness of her mother's equally fine and intelligent ones.

After a while the general came in. He is an entirely different type, with long, thin, strong but sensitive, scholarly face. I felt that he had a keenly analytical mind, and could combine philosophy with action. He listened sympathetically to my story and said it was a lot of damn nonsense, and I had better talk to Madame Chiang. Phoebe told him why Ch'u Djang thought it better to try to settle it from the bottom first, and he agreed. He said he would find out what we need to know, and telephone about it later.

Then I hastened to the embassy. Edith fell on my neck and nearly broke my glasses. One of the men who used to know me was standing by, and he said the same thing everyone else is saying—how much better I look than when I was here.

I guess maybe I am better, in spite of the gum infection. I've kept myself so tired by overwork that I scarcely realized my general health had improved. I remember now that I felt livelier as soon as I got to Kweiyang. The climate is much more pleasant, and although we have had lots of alarms, they just mean walking out into the mountains instead of spending hours in a dark cave. Having the periodontal disease cleared up by the dentist is making a wonderful difference. If I weren't better than last summer I couldn't dream of doing half of what I'm doing.

I had a great time with Edith and Helen. They are getting a bit fed up with the embassy. Security is tighter, so they have to teach in some damp rooms down by the gate instead of going to people's offices as we used to. When winter came the man in charge of lessons didn't provide stoves for them in those cold rooms, until in desperation Edith mentioned the matter to the ambassador, who does still have his lesson in his office. The next day they had stoves and the first man was in a pout. Then he said that they must always take substitute pupils if their regulars didn't come. Edith offered a compromise by which if someone were going to be absent for several days she would take a substitute. Helen objected even to that, saying her load was too heavy, and if she didn't have a free hour now and then she would have to cut down her number of pupils. The man said then that Helen needn't take substitutes, but Edith must in all her free hours. Edith went to the ambassador again, and the man got squelched again. He is leaving soon, and someone else will be in charge of lessons. It's quite a change from the relaxed atmosphere when I was there.

After lunch I walked through the town and bought a pair of cloth shoes ($5) and an eraser ($1) and went to the China Travel Service to see about having my suitcase sent over. They said it will be four days, as tomorrow is Chinese New Year, and they'll have three days off. So through the holiday, when everyone is supposed to wear new clothes, I'll wear my old, burned, padded gown and wash my underwear every night.

So home to Phoebe's, and Edith came and stayed for supper and we had a fine talk. She is now required to submit lesson plans for three months ahead for each of her pupils. I'm glad there was no such nonsense when I was there.

Journal, Chungking, February 10, 1940

Chang Tze-chung telephoned that the arrest warrant had not come from the generalissimo's staff. He would inquire next whether or not it came from the military tribunal.

It was a day of quiet, pleasant sociability at Phoebe's.

Part of long letter to Wally, Chungking, February 13, 1940

The order came from the military tribunal, and various approaches are being made. Chang Tze-chung gave your name to the head man with a request that the order be recalled or otherwise dropped. Wang Tze-wei and Dean King have close connections with General Ho, head of the court, and they will have him approached by his intimate friends. Mr. Wang has written to President Ou to suggest that the university send a petition to the court. You might make sure he received the letter.

Wang Tze-wei met Colonel Huang at a party and spoke about you. J. L. answered that the matter is out of his hands now. He can have nothing further to do with it.

Journal, Kweiyang, March 9, 1940

The rest of the time in Chungking was too crowded and confused for writing. Chang Tze-chung found that the order came from the military court. We had the university send a petitiion to the court. The general in charge said that as far as he was concerned the case was clear, but to make it all regular he must have a letter from Wally stating his reasons for leaving New Life. To save time I wrote the letter for Wally and had C. C. Liang translate it. Phoebe and I spent all Saturday afternoon looking for the court, getting there at ten minutes to five. A friend of hers who was expecting us rang bells and sent servants running to tell some men not to go home just yet. He took my letter to General Ho, came back, and wrote out an order recalling the arrest warrant. He said it would still have to pass through several hands and have the Generalissimo's seal, and might take some weeks to reach Kweiyang, but I could go back and tell the police it was on the way.

∾

I didn't get back to Kweiyang until February 24, two days before the new semester began.

I had tried to think of Colonel Huang not as an ogre, but as a harried human being. To my amazement he came to see me. We had a good talk, and came to understand that the root of the trouble between him and Wally lay even farther back than either of us had known, with Frank begging a job for his little brother.

Everyone in Chungking knew that those warrants were nonsense. No one tried to enforce them. People on the list were meeting the colonel every day. Why did I make a fuss about it? I said the police in Kweiyang didn't know it was a joke.

Some friend got me a free ride back to Kweiyang on a bus belonging to the Central Bank, which was hauling several chests of new banknotes to meet the demand of the rapid inflation. There were eight passengers. When we got into the mountains the chests kept trying to slide down on us. Everyone else seemed to be bothered by motion sickness or gasoline fumes, so I was the one to brace my feet against the backs of the seats, hold on to something in the top of the bus, and lean back against the chests hour after hour. I had to show that the foreigner could not only do the job, but do it with grace.

Chapter 19

In May, 1940, Wally was required to attend a political education camp for college professors in Chungking. He went sullenly, as all the others did, knowing that they would be lectured endlessly about Kuomintang orthodoxy, and warned to be alert for any signs of subversive thoughts on the part of their students.

A few days before he left we entered a period of persistent air raid alarms. People seemed more frightened by them than they had ever been before. They must have thought, as I did, that after the scouting plane that criss-crossed over us the other day, the next time might be business.

I kept a play-by-play account of the period, of which I will tell only two days.

Journal, Kweiyang, May 5, 1940

Yesterday I had a long, hot walk home after the last alarm, and then got busy covering a light blanket to look like a quilt for Wally to take with him. The regulations call for a quilt, and ours would be too warm. It isn't smart to show any signs of non-conformity. His other last-minute preparations kept us busy until midnight. I am to take over his Business English class.

This morning we were up at five-thirty to get his things checked in time to go on the same bus. I went to the station with him. The departure time had been changed from eight to seven-twenty to get it out as far ahead of alarms as possible. Sheng K'e-fei, director of Central Hospital and our old house-mate, was going too. As the bus pulled out, the street light by the station came on, the sign that planes have left their base but aren't near enough for an alarm. At night the lights are turned off for the same purpose.

People were already beginning to swarm out of the city. Another plane was circling around, perhaps preparing a bombing map, but we didn't get an alarm for it. I saw an officer looking at it with binoculars, and asked him whose plane it was.

"Yours," he said.

"What do you mean by that?"

"Japanese."

"Then don't call it mine."

"I beg your pardon, but it couldn't be up there without your country's gasoline."

That is a very sore point with us. Why does America continue to supply Japan with aviation gas and scrap iron?

It was useless to go to school. I was too tired to think straight, and hadn't prepared my lessons. I decided to pack a knapsack so as to carry more things than usual with me, and then type out carbon copies for the French class, so if the alarm hadn't come by ten-thirty I could meet them.

At ten-ten it did come. I went out a little farther than yesterday, to a sheltered, shady place, and settled down to write a letter home. After a bit we heard bombers, and the guards called out, "Planes coming! Don't move, don't talk."

I lay on my face between two little mounds, and put my notebook over my neck. There was a little anti-aircraft fire and then silence. I thought, what they must want most in Kweichow is lines of communication. I wonder if Wally's bus hasn't just about reached the big bridge? I tried not to think it.

Later, twelve-twenty—Clear signal. Go home for a nap.

Journal, Kweiyang, May 6, 1940

Yesterday afternoon I rested a while and began getting organized for a month of widowhood. The street lights were on all day, and in the evening they were turned off. The Japanese must be really buzzing around.

They say there were two hundred killed in a place fifty miles from here. That's probably exaggerated, as first reports always are. One bomb fell five miles from Kweiyang, but didn't hit anyone. Three people were wounded by machine gun fire near the Central Hospital.

This morning I met my French class at eight. I took up the advanced lesson first instead of the review drill, because the lights were already on. Soon the sirens were whooping it up, and I came out with my four best students to a place which is good except for a lot of thorny slash on the ground and a bad-tempered farm woman who thinks we will spoil her vegetables. She railed to high heaven, scolding us for talking. The country people believe that if you talk it will attract the bombs. Someone pointed out that she was talking louder than any of us, but she yelled, "If I don't talk, you'll have all my cabbages ruined."

Later—The urgent alarm had scarcely sounded when we heard planes. There was a little anti-aircraft fire, once so close that we put our notebooks over our heads for fear of falling stuff. Once we heard what might have been a distant bomb.

Later, ten-ten—Clear signal, but I'm so comfortable here that I'm going to stay and correct my French notebooks. There will probably be another alarm.

Later, one p.m.—I finished my notebooks and then went home for lunch. I was afraid if I didn't go the girls would wait for me until too late to eat their own lunch. I washed up and had a few bites before the alarm came again. I fed the dogs and brought Jeannie out with me.

I am in a very good place, a hedge with gravemounds on either side, and two friendly soldiers for company. They asked why I didn't go back to America and get away from all this. I had time to clear away the thorn branches and make a snug nest for myself before the planes came. There seemed to be a lot of them this time, and lots of bombs, though not close by.

Later—I had just settled down for a nap when the clear signal came. I decided to stay until there was less chance of another siren. I placed my briefcase for a pillow and the typewriter beside it, and slept with the basket handle and Jeannie's leash in my hand. Jeannie slept quietly beside me.

Jeannie is a very good dog, but she is so afraid of the siren that we just have to take her out with us if we are at home when the alarm comes. When we can, we take both dogs. But I can't manage two with my other load when I'm alone. Bobby just has to stay alone. At the first note of the siren, before we can even hear it, Jeannie runs to us and whines and bounces. When the planes come she cowers against us. You wouldn't know her then for the valorous Scottie who hunts rats at all hours of the night. She and her offspring are the only Scotties Kweiyang has ever seen. When we take her out we hear great arguments about whether she is a dog at all. Some call her a wolf-dog, and others say she is a dog-bear, whatever that may be. Total strangers, from rickshaw pullers to elegant young men, perceiving her to be a mother, ask for one of her pups. The present puppies (unplanned parenthood) are a strange lot, but all are promised to people of substance.

Later—It's about three, and I'm going home.

Evening—I've done little the past two days, but I'm deathly tired. When I came home I rested a bit and started putting things in order, and then a long distance call came.

It was Sheng K'e-fei. When the bus reached Kikiang there was a telegram saying that the Central Hospital had been bombed, six wards destroyed and six nurses killed. Wally was trying to call me to see if I was safe, but he'd gone to do something while waiting for the call, so Coffee talked to me instead. He asked me to get in touch with Gertrude Pao (head of the nursing school), tell her he was starting back right away, and ask her to wire details to him at Tung-tze where he could get them on the way back.

I telephoned the hospital and finally got Gertrude on the line. The connection was bad, so I didn't try to get details, but just gave the message. I asked, "Are you all right?"

"Not all right. I'm not hurt, but it's terrible."

She sounded so tired I wanted to cry for her. She said there was nothing I could do to help, so I hung up and tried not to think about it.

I got busy washing a lot of clothes that had been soaking since the day before. I had to stop in the middle for supper and finish by the light of a kerosene lamp. (We wash clothes in the courtyard.) I haven't given the girls lessons all week, but my brain was too tired for teaching. The manual work of washing was just what I needed to put me to sleep.

Jounrnal, Kweiyang, June, 1940

A couple of days later I had a chance to talk with Dr. Phil Greene, who was at the Central Hospital the day of the bombing. He said only four girls were killed, and two wounded. There were many bombs around the hospital, but only one struck the building. It was in the staff dining room.

The nurses had just come off duty and were dead tired. At the urgent alarm the man whose duty it is to see that people get out came and urged them to go. They said they were too tired to move, and anyway they didn't think it was any safer outside than in. As soon as the planes were gone Dr. Greene rushed back and found the mess. The other nurses came back and went into hysterics. It was pretty awful.

Every patient who could move at all left the hospital, so they haven't much to do now except get reorganized.

Through the month of May Julia, who is a Chungking girl, read me the reports from the Chinese paper about the persistent bombing around Chungking. From one to two hundred planes a day were dropping incendiary bombs all around the suburbs, where everything important has gone. One night she told me an official report that was not supposed to be made public, that ten thousand people had been killed within a few days.

When the numbers get so big, one's brain simply refuses to handle them. It just registers the round number without dwelling on details. Each individual casualty is such a pitiful story that the human mind cannot bear to picture what thousands of them really mean. After a little bombing such as we had, with about thirty casualties, people discuss the individual cases: why didn't those nurses take shelter? Why was that man's head blown off when his family members were safe? But when it begins to run into hundreds people don't even ask where the bombs hit, beyond making sure that their homes and friends are safe.

There are women on the crews of Japanese bombers now. Recently one was brought down and the crew taken alive. Two of the five were women.

Letter, Kweiyang, June 1, 1940
Dear Folks,

I have resolved to write short letters more often instead of long ones now and then. That way there may be more chance that some will come through.

Before I forget, I want to ask you to send a Vogue pattern book, or whatever kind you can get. Anything within a couple of years is fine unless there has been a radical change. The best foreign-style ladies' tailor in Kweiyang has only a few pages out of a catalog of things for outsize women for ideas to copy.

I've just had a scrappy note from Wally, the first in more than two weeks. He had warned me he wouldn't have time to write. He says, "I'll try to be home before the tenth. We have had too many alarms lately. Each time we have to climb a high hill to get into the cave, and stay there for three to six hours. We don't get enough sleep. The food in the camp is not sufficient at all. I am becoming like a spoiled child, wanting some extra all the time. My money is getting less and less. I'll have to borrow if I don't get a free ride to Kweiyang."

The girls are gone except Mary, and we have taken over the house. I like my new helper. She feeds us better than the cook did, and washes and cleans besides. I had a party for five foreigners one day. I was going to have food sent in, but she said she could manage. Blessed if she didn't do us proud! If I cook something myself she doesn't just go off and sleep, as the cook did, but watches so she will know how to do it next time.

I wonder what is happening to all my European friends. I have (or had) friends in France, Belgium, Holland, Norway, Denmark, Czechoslovakia and Poland, to mention only those who have war in their midst. And I'm just as sorry for the Germans and Italians, but I've always been sorry for them anyway. When I think of all the little boys I knew, who are military age now, it makes me sick.

The university is pressing me to teach full time next year, but I am determined not to. I want to have time to make a baby. Of course it will be hard to make ends meet on one salary, but if I can sell even a little writing in America it will more than make up the difference.

Love to all,

Letter, Kweiyang, June 14, 1940

Dear Folks,

Just one more week of classes and Wally and I can, for the first time ever, have a summer vacation together. We had two summers in Chungking, but no vacation.

We are saddened these days by the news from Europe and also by Japan's renewed determination to wipe out the city of Chungking. After June of last year they never bombed inside the city until this month, but now they are carrying out a deliberate campaign of destruction. The Soviet Embassy was hit the other day, and many other places that we knew. They are sending over one hundred planes a day now. Somebody heard on the radio that Ichang has fallen. If so it will be easier for them to fly to Chungking.

Julia had word that her eleven-year-old sister was killed at a place about one hundred miles from Chungking. It wasn't made clear why the girl hadn't taken cover, but the probable explanation is that they were so used to seeing the planes go by to Chungking that they quit paying attention to them. More than three hundred were killed in that place that day, which can only mean that people in general didn't take refuge.

People can't make a living while sitting in a shelter day after day, and it's hard to enforce the discipline even on children when you know that the planes are going to Chungking, and that if by chance they are driven off from there, there's only a small chance that they will choose the spot where you are to drop their bombs.

Wally and I insist on shelter discipline for our household. You can never know when they will come your way. A plane loaded with bombs cannot land safely, so once it takes the air it must drop its bombs somewhere.

I hate to think of America getting involved in the war in Europe. I'd rather think that her role is to remain sane in the midst of a world gone crazy, but I would be more sure of my country's sanity if she would stop providing Japan with the scrap iron and aviation gasoline, without which this bombing would be impossible.

Wally got back last Sunday, disgusted with the propaganda he had been subjected to. He's having a strenuous time trying to condense his lectures enough to cover the ground in the few days left before examinations. He has classes from six in the morning every day, but it will soon be over.

All three dogs are enthusiastic ratters now—a blessing.

Love to all,

Chapter 20

Through July, 1940 we continued to have many alarms and occasional raids, so that we spent much of our summer vacation sitting in favorite spots in the mountains. My journal states simply that I signed up for full time teaching for the following year. There is no record of any struggle about it. I probably did it willingly. I would no longer have the girls to teach, and I would have eight hours of French, which I liked, and four hours of sophomore English, which should not be too bad. My many days of sick leave without pay had made full time seem more attractive.

Wally and I made a new policy about air raids. We had thought it was better to be together, so that if one were killed we both might be. We came to realize that wounding is much more likely than killing, and that if one were hurt it would be good for the other to be able to take charge.

I packed two trunks for Wally to take to Hua-ch'i to store at Sheng Chih-yuan's house. I tried to include the most valuable things, and also what we could spare of everyday necessities that we would need at once if everything else was lost. There was no way to secure the typewriter and the books, on which our work depended. We had to have them for constant use, but if they were burned we'd be done for. We put them in the gatehouse, which was isolated, with brick on two sides, and so comparatively safe from fire.

I found a good Chinese teacher, Miss Ch'u of the radio station, with whom I traded lessons three times a week. Not only was her diction very clear and precise, but she knew phonetics and could help me with the sounds that are not like English.

Journal, Kweiyang, Monday July 15, 1940

I'm afraid the baby we had hope of for two weeks is spoiled. I sent my teacher away this morning and have been lying as still as I can in the hope of saving it. I had a picnic lunch ready to take if there were an alarm, so I wouldn't have to run back and forth, but now it's one o'clock and I've eaten it. It seems too fine a day not to have an alarm. I've felt very tired all day.

Journal, Kweiyang, July 16, 1940

Today is cloudy enough to give hope of peace. I've kept as quiet as I could, but I had to get up to help Wally train the dogs not to bother chickens. He had bought two half-grown ones and we had a wild time, feathers and fur flying. At last I held Bobby and Wally held a chicken, and we let the chicken peck Bobby until he was thoroughly frightened, I hope it works.

Journal, Kweiyang, July 19, 1940

It was a miscarriage. Something was expelled last night that was definitely not just blood clot. This morning I tracked down Dr. Louise Li of Kweiyang Medical College. She said it sounded like a miscarriage, but she would examine it microscopically to make sure. She thought it likely that my two previous experiences were miscarriages, too. She gave me ergot and said to keep up calcium and halibut oil and to rest in bed a lot. After the bleeding stops she will see what must be done to give me better luck next time.

Journal, Kweiyang, July 20, 1940

I had my Chinese lesson and lay down to rest, but Wally brought home five more chickens that had to be introduced to the dogs. Miss Clark came by and read me the riot act for being up and around so soon after a miscarriage. Dr. Li had told me to rest, but hadn't exactly said I shouldn't get up at all. She said for me to lie on my tummy for an hour twice a day, and the rest of the time I could be propped up to read. It's hard for a woman to rest in her own home.

Journal, Kweiyang, July 21, 1940

Dr. Emma Tucker came over. Mary had seen her on the street and asked her to come. She is pleased to find that I am in the hands of Louise Li, for whom she has great respect, but she was horrified at my being out of bed at all for a week after the event. She said that, according to her experience, if I tried again within a year I would almost certainly miscarry again.

She told me about a man (Mr. Coberly?) who is taking a Seventh Day Adventist truck to somewhere near Shanghai, leaving tomorrow and expecting to return at once. He might be able to bring in French books for me. I went to Tuckers' to see him and he said he'd be glad to do it. I asked for twelve first-year books because I hadn't the nerve to ask for more. I must get dictionaries and second year books some other way. It will be great if I don't have to make up my own lessons and type carbons for everyone.

Journal, Kweiyang, July 27, 1940

While I was at the hospital for my treatment there was an alarm which we could scarcely hear because the electricity was off and they had to use a little hand-crank siren. She showed me the hospital shelter, which even has a delivery table in it. Since no one else could come, we had a long talk, and she told me more about miscarriages than she could if there were patients waiting.

The reason she is willing for me to try again right away is that we can't be sure the first two occasions were miscarriages. If I really do have a miscarriage habit, I may miscarry again in spite of anything we can do, and if that happens she would advise waiting a year. Since we weren't sure, she thought it worth while to go ahead and see if we can pull the next one through. She said I am not likely to conceive soon with my cervix in the condition it is. She wants to treat it daily for a long time.

It seems we were very foolish about this pregnancy. Because I was sure the baby was spoiled, I kept getting up for all kinds of things. I should have had sedatives, and lain flat for two weeks after the bleeding stopped. It's as if there were a wound that had to be held shut in order to heal, but they can't get in there to sew it up.

Journal, Kweiyang, July 28, 1940

I came out early to a trench beside the path, with Jeannie, Bobby, a brief case, and a bag of things to work on. Wally went to Hua-ch'i in a Red Cross truck with two suitcases to store at the Sheng's. Other people have come into the trench. I invited a woman with a baby to share my oilcloth, and when the planes were near I gave her a notebook to hold over the baby's head. Planes circled around for about fifteen minutes, dropping a few bombs.

The trench reminds me of the one we had in Nanking. It has only a screen of branches over it, and nothing to sit on, while in Nanking we had little chairs, and there was a roof of timbers with earth piled over them. What struck me as I thought about it was that Frank said he would plant trees over it in the spring to hide it. How funny to think we never doubted that we would still be there in the spring!

Evening—At T'u Yung Kwan, some miles from here, the Chinese Red Cross was bombed and a lot of wounded soldiers wounded again.

There was a rumor that Yale-in-China and other American property would be destroyed today to frighten America out of cutting off war supplies to Japan. Japanese radio often makes such announcements to upset people. Sometimes the threat is made good, and sometimes not.

Journal, Kweiyang, July 28, 1940

Mrs. Wang Po-ch'un (the president's wife) and her sister came to see me. They brought me two tins of sweetened condensed milk and two of pineapple—rare treats. When they were gone I opened one of the cans of milk and ate half of it right down with a spoon, feeling a little ashamed as I did so. Now the can is empty. What a pig!

Today I read in the Hankow Herald (the only English paper we have now) that the U.S. is stopping the shipment of oil and scrap iron to Japan. I felt a glow of hope that Japan would no longer be able to squander such things on civilians. For a moment I even dared to imagine an end to the war, but when I read on I saw that the U.S. is taking this step, not out of any feeling for us in China, but because she is afraid of needing all her war materials for herself. When I read in the next column that Congress is pushing through a compulsory military training law, and that the War Department is ready to draft an army of one hundred forty thousand men as soon as the law is passed, I really felt gloomy. There is strong opposition in the Senate to a peace-time military draft. One of the reasons my groszvater brought his family to America was to save them from the compulsory military service he had known in his youth.

We haven't had alarms the past couple of days. Dr. Li still wants me to spend several hours a day in knee-chest position, and go to her most days for treatment of my eroded cervix.

Chapter 21

Journal, Kweiyang, Friday, August 2, 1940

The weather has been lovely, changing all the time from showers to clear, with great cumulus clouds tumbling around, always pleasant, never hot, and seldom settled enough for air raids.

The raid last Monday was bad. They dropped three bombs on a concentration of one hundred fifty new government trucks and damaged about half of them beyond repair. The rest can be patched up using parts from the wrecked ones. The person in charge says he didn't disperse them when the alarm came because he had no gasoline, but he still has to explain why he had so many in one place. That kind of loss is serious, but that kind of incompetence is all too common.

Mary, the last one of our girls, has her orders to leave, and is busy preparing. She has two supposedly foreign-style skirts of blue serge, one cotton and one nice wool, which she loves to wear. They give me the willies because they are so badly made—just straight lengths of cloth pleated and darted any old way to make the waistline somewhere near the right size so they can be pinned to fit. Long ago I promised her that I'd recut them for her in my summer vacation. Today she asked if I had time. Of course I must do it. We both ripped away until dark, producing clear pieces of cloth which she washed so I can cut them out in the morning.

Journal, Kweiyang, August 5, 1940

Miss Ch'u didn't come for her lesson, so I used the time to cut Mary's skirt. She is so fat that she can use my pattern by shortening the skirt about six inches and the waistband four. She took my old green seersucker to a tailor as a model for a dress.

The skirt cut with not an inch to spare. I had just got it pinned together when Tai T'sao-luan came and stayed all morning drilling the French sentences I had given him.

Journal, Kweiyang, August 6, 1940

Mary's skirt fits well. She can have a tailor make the second one like it. Still great weather—beautiful clouds day after day.

We thought we would have to get out of this house when Mary leaves, but today someone came to take the rest of the things the organization has here. He asked me to tell him when we find a place, so they can cancel the lease on this one. We immediately arranged to take it over ourselves. It's not perfect, but unusually good for Kweiyang. We won't have telephone and electricity anymore, but we have a box of candles that I bought in Chungking last year for $61.50. That will last most of the year when good light is important if we eke out with vegetable oil lamps. There's a huge room that we don't need. Maybe we can find a congenial person to sublet it.

Think of saving the labor and expense of moving in this last month of vacation! When the men were gone I celebrated by washing the living room windows. I had refrained from doing so because I thought we were going to move. It's nice to have them clean and to feel that this will be our home for a while longer.

Journal, Kweiyang, August 9, 1940

We were in the middle of our favorite lunch of noodles when there was an alarm, the first in more than a week. When it was over, Wally had to go at once because he was on the committee for the Y's Men's Club dinner. He hates that sort of thing, but got elected business manager and is in the thick of it.

I thought it best to go to the dinner myself, although I also dislike such things. I have no excuse not to go this time, and if I never go people will wonder why Wally keeps his wife out of sight. I made myself as beautiful as I could in the yellow and white dimity dress I made, which is the only new thing I have had this year.

There was a big crowd, packing the Student Relief Center social room— not only a big crowd, but a good crowd, all the people who matter. The program was rotten.

Wally was busy serving but I didn't care. There were lots of people I knew. I sat with Dr. Pai of the Hsiang Ya (Yale-in-China) medical college and we had a delightful discussion of guinea pigs.

Journal, Kweiyang, August 13, 1940

Dr. Li says I am no better. I must do more knee-chest position. I must not iron clothes because it keeps me on my feet too much. I certainly shouldn't have washed the windows the other day. I'll have to teach Li Sao, our current amah, to iron.

Letter, Kweiyang, August 17, 1940
Dear Folks,

Our lovely weather still holds. We've had only two raids and two false alarms in the past month. I spend hours on our veranda, from which I can see three little mountains and a jumble of half-timbered gables with tall trees standing up between, and a glorious expanse of sky. In the late afternoon I like to watch the big birds called kites playing on the thermals, gliding around without moving their wings. We think that in the future Kweichow will be a popular summer resort. You couldn't find a nicer climate. Before the war it was the poorest and most remote part of China, and few people thought of coming here.

The past few mornings have been so clear that we thought there must be a raid, but each time it clouded up. The Japanese had announced on the radio that they would come on the 13th, 14th, and 15th, but they didn't. They have a habit of making such announcements about one city or another, which are disturbing even when the raids do not happen.

Do you realize that I've been in China five years? It doesn't seem long to have been here, but it does seem a long time not to have been home. When I think of the little kids who are grown up, and of Father not teaching anymore, that's the kind of thing that makes it seem long.

Love to all,

Journal, Kweiyang, August 20, 1940

Dr. Li was still in the ward when the sirens sounded. She called to me to wait for my treatment, which takes only a minute. Then I went to our usual cemetery, and had just picked my spot when Wally came with two dogs. About ten-thirty, to the slow crescendo of approaching planes, I wormed myself down between two mounds. The bombs and anti-aircraft were popping for a while.

I have never since heard anything like what we sometimes heard in Nanking, when the heavens would be one rocking, swelling symphony of doom. It must have been so in Chungking, but there we were in deep caves.

Journal, Kweiyang, August 22, 1940

The Japanese continue to keep us out in the delightful countryside most of the time. The alarms have been coming very early. Wally has an infected foot, but I've been soaking it in water when I could, and it's getting better.

This morning Wally wanted to try going out early to a place he had heard of which is too far to go after the alarm. We walked to the Great West Gate, and out on the main road to a little tea house across from the February Fourth Factory, where they employ women left destitute by the February 4th bombing

or by having their husbands conscripted. He bought me a bowl of "sweet wine"
(fermented rice) with two eggs poached in it. Then we came on slowly, taking
the old stone road through the forest. I found myself enjoying a sense of holi-
day, with the balmy breeze, the blue-and-white sky, the green vistas of forest,
and the blue lines of hills far off. It's not at all like hurrying out among the
milling crowds after the alarm.

We are sitting at an open-air tea place under the trees. There are a good
many people here, but not a crowd. They seem carefree. You wouldn't dream that
they were hiding from danger. They seem more like Sunday promenaders in the
Black Forest except that they don't sing. There is little in sight that could not
be a poor part of the Black Forest, even the two thatched huts of stone and mud.
I feel relaxed and at peace.

Journal, Kweiyang, August 23, 1940

We came out the same way as yesterday. At an easy pace with no stops
it took forty-five minutes. We chose a soft, shady place on the forest floor, with
lush grass, near a stand of blue flowers, larger and shallower than a bluebell.
The trees around us are young pines. Near by are clumps of fern. Not far away
are poplars that glisten in the sun and whisper companionably in the breeze.
Wally is sleeping with my handkerchief over his eyes. A laughing family has
just settled down near us. It is idyllic.

I took a rickshaw home, and found I had missed a visit from John
Hlavacek, the Carleton-in-China man. We would have liked to see him. He
has driven all over Free China on IRC trucks.

Journal, Kweiyang, August 28, 1940

This morning I had to give a two-hour lecture on the teaching of Eng-
lish to a group of middle-school teachers, from six-thirty to eight-thirty. I got
up at four to put the finishing touches on my speech, which is a joke because I
never give the speech I planned. However, being prepared makes one better able
to improvise.

It was raining, so I took Wally's big rubber cape that he bought in Nanking
and set out for the Southwest Middle School, in the fields behind the Febru-
ary Fourth Factory. I got there just on time, really, but found that they keep
their clock half an hour slow to allow for speakers coming late.

The speech went off all right though it reminded me of the University of
Fribourg in Switzerland, where the lectures should have been called dictations,
with ample time between sentences for the students to write them down verba-
tim. I had been afraid I didn't have enough material, but it turned out to be

too much. I had to speak very slowly, and they kept asking me to repeat so they could get their notes down. Their notes have to be handed in to me to check over. When I finished they asked me to give them my notes, which I did.

Journal, August 29, 1940

Dr. Li was horrified at my condition. I have been much too active. She says a reasonable amount of walking is all right, but I've overdone it. I must avoid standing up a lot, as it's in standing still that congestion occurs.

Chapter 22

Journal, Kweiyang, Monday, September 2, 1940

I kept very quiet all day. Miss Ch'u taught me the Song of the Manchurian Refugees, and I've been singing it all afternoon as I lay on the bed mending Wally's sweater. I'm actually reweaving the elbows. That sweater should have been discarded a couple of years ago by any normal standards, but nowadays one expects clothes to be permanent.

Journal, Kweiyang, Tuesday, September 3, 1940

Dr. Li says I'm no better, and must still rest as much as possible. If I have my appendix done it will help, as I'll have to rest ten days after that. The appendix is chronic, just a nagging pain when I walk, so that I have to hug a book against it for support. It wouldn't merit surgery except for the possibility that it might become acute at a time when I was out of reach of modern medicine.

Coffee (Dr. Sheng K'e-fei), who will do the surgery if I have it, was here for supper. He had just driven down from Chungking. He said half of Chungking is so wiped out that you can't find any landmark to show where you are. He thinks there can't be a house in the city that hasn't at least had its windows broken. Rice is $250 a tan (about one hundred and fifty pounds). The servants in his hospital (he is head of the Central Hospital branch there as well as here), pay six k'uai a month for their food, which is so far from covering even the cost of the rice that the hospital subsidizes their dining room to the extent of four k'uai per person. With this they have barely adequate rice and very little vegetable. They complain about only one thing: They want more salt. When Coffee heard this he ordered that they have all the salt they want, and ten catties (about fifteen pounds) a month of meat. He'll find the money somewhere.

Journal, Kweiyang, Wednesday, September 3, 1940

An alarm came early. We were back by a little after ten. About eleven there was a new alarm. We were just locking the door upstairs when we saw a plane, quite low, speeding very black against low clouds. It was less than five minutes after the alarm. There was a sound like a bomb, and a lot of anti-air-

craft fire. We wouldn't be allowed to move in the street, so we sat on the stone stools by the gatehouse. The popping went on for a few minutes, and then I went up to do my knee-chest.

In five minutes the urgent alarm sounded. We went into the gatehouse where our precious things are stored, and sat on low stools behind a pile of boxes. Just after noon several planes came, circled around for a while, and went away, only to return and circle again. The clouds were a good deal heavier and lower than when the first plane came, so I suppose they couldn't find their objective and the Archies couldn't find them. We felt a little uneasy when they kept circling, as when they can't find their target they may just unload their bombs anywhere. Soon they were gone and nothing had happened, though there was no clear signal. A strange performance.

Journal, Kweiyang, Thursday, September 5, 1940

Wally bought a pig's head to try head cheese. It boiled tender overnight, and I helped Li Sao cut up the meat. I seasoned it and told her how to proceed. We used the ears to make noodles for breakfast, as we wanted a substantial meal before going out for the day. We had heard that thirty-six planes came yesterday, couldn't find the city, and bombed Lungli on the way back. As we had never had more than nine before, it seemed as if the big one might be coming.

At eight we had just reached the main street (P'u T'ing Lu) when the sirens sounded. People seemed excited. Many were running, carrying more stuff than usual. We went out through the village and took the old stone road to the mountains, then in among the hills and up a little valley. We found a fine hiding place, full of gullies, springs and caves. Lots of other people were going that far too, and going briskly.

We found a dry gully full of long grass, well up the mountain, over-looking the city. There we made ourselves a snug nest, protected on all sides and screened from above by overhanging grasses. Wally dozed and I knitted and the two dogs snoozed in their own nests until the all clear.

We stayed where we were, and at noon there was another alarm. By that time the clouds were thick enough to protect us, and it didn't last long. After two o'clock we started back slowly. We met the Ch'ao family, whose trench we have shared so often. They also had come out farther than usual.

Mr. Ch'ao, who has something to do with air defense, said that yesterday one hundred eight planes tried to come here from Hankow, but were turned back by the rain. They came in waves of thirty-six. That is disturbing news. The planes that have come here before were navy planes from Nanning

(Kwangsi) and have behaved very well, aiming at military targets. It is possible to believe that when they hit the Central Hospital they were aiming at the arsenal, and when they hit the Chinese Red Cross at T'uyungkwan they were trying for the Southwest Transport Company. They never came in large numbers, and they always sent scouts to prepare the bombing map. That may be more deadly from a military standpoint than promiscuous bombing, but at least it gives civilians a fair chance.

These army planes from Hankow are another story. They are the ones that have wiped out the city of Chungking this summer, and have bombed civilians disastrously in many other places, including killing Julia's sister. In and around Chungking they have often attacked universities and missions. Since June it has been clear that their objective was the systematic razing of the city. Recently they dropped leaflets in Chungking saying that when they finished that job they would wipe out Chengtu and Kweiyang. A broadcast from Tokyo recently said that Kweiyang's turn was coming soon. The commander of the Hankow airfield is notorious for choosing any and all but military objectives. Their planes are better than the Kwangsi ones, too. Mr. Ch'ao explained all this, and we resolved to be more careful from now on.

One hundred eight planes raiding Kweiyang would compare to a thousand for Chungking. The disastrous bombing of February 4, 1939, which wiped out the whole center of the city, was the work of nine planes with incendiaries.

Journal, Kweiyang, Friday, September 6, 1940

I got to Dr. Li at her home last evening. She was in a Japanese kimono, eating ti lo pu. She thought I had better postpone my wisdom tooth extractions. When I left her I went by Haywards to make sure they knew about the change in the air raid prospects, as Eve is expecting a baby in November.

Journal, Kweiyang, Saturday, September 7, 1940

This morning was cloudy enough to seem safe. Wally went to school early and I settled down to work in bed. Then something said, "Don't be a fool. Get up." I had just time to get dressed before the alarm came at eight-fifteen. I went out with the two dogs and the briefcase to a cemetery beyond the village, and stayed there until the all-clear. Then I looked for a shadier place, and decided the place where we were last time was best. As I started up the valley a girl said, "Don't go up there alone. There's a bad man up there who robs people." I said I wasn't afraid because my dogs were very fierce, but I found a place within earshot of her party.

Someone in the air defense told Wally that when the one hundred eight planes came it was to drop parachutists. Mechanized troops have been rushed here in case they try it again. That would explain why I saw big, black "chevaux de Frise" piled by the gate. These are things with sharp points in every direction, used originally as a defense against cavalry.

The day they failed to find us they bombed Yuanling badly on the way back. That's where Wally's parents are. Someone we know happened to be in the air defense tracking station in Chungking, where they watch where the bombers are going. They gazed in horror as the planes approached us, saying, "Ai-ya! Kweiyang is done for!"

Journal, Kweiyang, Thursday, September 12, 1940

Got up early and wondered why I was utterly faint with hunger. I decided it was probably a touch of morning sickness. I peeled a couple of ti lo pu and lay down to eat them. Breakfast didn't make me feel better.

Dr. Tucker heard that the Japanese have blown up the railroad bridge at the Indo-China border. That may mean no more mail coming up by train from Haiphong to Kunming.

Wally went out to get a suitcase of things that Bill sent from Kunming. Such riches! Ten French texts and six dictionaries for my second year class, a pound of calcium lactate (worth $22 here now), two shirts for Wally, a pound of surgical gauze for diapers, two rolls of adhesive plaster, a typewriter ribbon, a tin of Del Monte jam, a pound tin of French butter, and a Max Factor lipstick. The last is in a color I can't possibly wear, but it will be a suitable gift for Mrs. Wang Po-chun. Oh, yes, there was a bedsheet too.

Journal, Kweiyang, Saturday, September 14, 1940

When I got home from the alarm yesterday, Wally was already here and had some food ready: rice and under-done pumpkin and burned beef with green beans. I choked some down and rested a while, and then he came up with a huge dish of Chinese fried chicken with sweet peppers. Our biggest rooster had had an accident, and had to be killed. Such chicken! Fat and delicious, better than any we have bought for a long time. It seemed terrible to sit and wolf it down all by ourselves, but what else could we do? I was hungry, and it did hit the spot.

We keep having alarms every day. Now I'm sitting in a pleasant place and Wally has gone back to town. People are working on the rice harvest near by. There's a sound of mountain water on both sides of me. Men come to fill buckets at the spring. People come to drink. Farmers go by with bill hooks and sickles, and Miao tribal women come down the mountain with loads of dry grass or twigs on their backs, their blue kilts swinging as they walk.

Later—Wally heard that the scouting plane the other day dropped leaflets saying we mustn't suppose they couldn't find us the day the many planes came. It was just that they were very humane and didn't want to kill a lot of people, so they were giving us plenty of warning. It said they will come tomorrow and bomb the city.

If they are so humane, why did they bomb the guts out of Yuanling and Chikiang on the way back that day, and come back a few days later to finish off those two places?

Journal, Kweiyang, Monday, September 16, 1940

Mid-autumn festival. No alarm today. Li Sao said T'ien Fu (Heaven Father) gave us peace for the festival. I wonder about her concept of T'ien Fu. Miss Ch'u brought a gift of walnuts and pomegranates. I had a luxurious day at home, heightened by the half-expectation of an alarm any minute. Wally had invited the shop students for supper. After eating we sat on the veranda to admire the moon, which is the central theme of the festival. We nibbled mooncakes (round cakes with a rich sweet or spicy stuffing) and drank hot water.

Journal, Kweiyang, Tuesday, September 17, 1940

There was an alarm before breakfast. When it was over I went to T'ung Shan T'ai to buy bread. At Le Ch'un Men (Happy Crowds Gate) there were many guards and lots of "chevaux de Frise." They must be taking the threat of parachutists seriously.

I went home, got a big drink of water, and cut up a loaf of bread to dry so as to have something to nibble before I get up in the morning to settle my stomach. Then there was another alarm, and afterward I slept.

Journal, Kweiyang, Thursday, September 19, 1940

I had my first letter from home in nearly three months. It had a picture of Mother and Dad.

A lovely day, with big, turbulent clouds and no alarm.

Dr. Li said I was much better, and probably pregnant. She gave me some medicine. When I said how utterly useless I am she said, "Just remember you are doing something inside, and don't fret if you can't do two things at once." She thinks I can have my teeth out next week, but the appendix must wait until the fifth month. She wishes I could wait until the third month to start teaching, but I don't see how I can do that when I'll have to stop early in the spring, too. I'd be happy not to teach at all, but the contract is signed. I may be able to find a substitute for the English, but never for the French.

We almost forgot to go to a wedding at a swank new restaurant. The man is making a study of Miao dialects. He is marrying a middle school girl of a rich family. It was a very big and expensive party. The bride went through the ceremony wearing an elegant dress of flowered transparent velvet, and then changed for the feast into a still more elegant dress of the most vivid red. Some people can still live like that . . .

∾

Abrupt end of the Kweiyang diaries.

Chapter 23

Although Dr. Li disapproved, I had no choice but to teach when school opened. I said I would only go to class and spend the rest of the time in bed.

After a few days as I was walking home I felt a gush of blood. Was it worse to walk the rest of the way, or to jolt in a rickshaw? I chose to walk. At home I lay flat on the bed until Wally could get word to Dr. Li. She sent men with a stretcher to take me to the hospital.

If you have never ridden on a stretcher carried by men who don't synchronize their steps—don't!

The hospital was a large, thatched, mud-walled structure with a cotton cloth ceiling to keep scorpions from falling on the beds. The floor was tamped earth. For staff there were doctors from the Yale-in-China medical college (Hsiang Ya). All the nurses were trained midwives, competent to handle any but extreme emergencies. The head nurse was a very starchy graduate of the Peiping Union Medical College, who would not brook any compromise with primitive conditions.

I was placed in a horizontal position and held there by sandbags for two weeks, disturbed only by essential nursing care. I have no memory of how I managed to blank my mind to make this tolerable, but I know I was given sedatives. My baby was at stake, and I would do whatever I had to do. After two weeks I was allowed up, and gradually resumed normal living. The pregnancy progressed without further incident unless you count the time in the eighth month when I jumped down a six-foot bank into a rice paddy to avoid being bowled over by a galloping pack horse.

Letter, Kweiyang, November 19, 1940
Dear Folks,

It's nearly a month since I sent Mother a note from the hospital. You will be glad to know that I did not lose the baby, and am now fine. I'll soon be able to start teaching, one class at a time. If all goes well we expect Frederick or Margaret about the middle of May.

We heard last night that the Japanese hijacked a shipment of American Flying Fortresses on its way to China. The person who told us said that the first time they used them they brought down eight of the eighteen Chinese fighters that went up to meet them. All units of the Chinese Air Force have been ordered to turn tail when they see these things until we can get some fighters capable of dealing with them.

The Americans here (about fifteen) are going to pool their resources to achieve a Thanksgiving dinner. Knowing that I have to spare myself, they didn't put me down to contribute anything, but I insisted on at least making candy and salted peanuts. We'll meet at Tuckers' and Mrs. Tucker will provide roast goose and mince pie. Another person who has an oven will make pumpkin pie. The last potatoes of the season are still available. If anybody made redfruit jelly it will do for cranberry sauce. Among the lot of us we should whomp up a pretty good feast.

I really have very little to do with other foreigners. Their lifestyle seems unrealistic to me. I like some of them very much as people, but don't seem to have much in common with them. The Tuckers are both doctors, and used to know brother Frank in Peiping back in the twenties.

If any of you write a letter that isn't up to weight it would be fine to enclose a few sheets of carbon paper. A little came from Father, and some from Abby Merritt in the Carleton office, who was perceptive enough to see my need. If you know that I write much of my lesson material as I go along, making carbons for the students, you can see that this is important. The school office will stencil anything I ask them to, but the stencils are handwritten by students who don't understand the material, and printed on rough, brittle paper, so they are scarcely legible.

I don't know what is happening to letters now. For about three weeks last summer, when the Hong Kong-Haiphong route was first interrupted, no one had any home mail. Then a lot of things came at once, and then nothing. Now we hear there are four ships a month from New York around South Africa to Rangoon (thirty-six days), so mail should come all right, though slowly. I don't know whether you get my letters.

We wonder a lot about the future, and about whether Em and her kids are on their way home for a visit. I'd rather be here, if communications are cut off, but for her it's different. In case of trouble where she is it would mean being interned with the kids. I know America as a whole still doesn't want to fight, but can they avoid it at the pace things are going?

I suppose most Americans, like myself, have wished to think of their country as an island of sanity in a crazy world, but I see I must give up any such illusion. Peace is not a right to be claimed, but a reward to be earned, and America has not earned it. She refused to pay the price after the First World War, when she imposed a vindictive settlement, and scuttled the League of Nations. In that way she contributed to the social disintegration leading to the present chaos.

When Japan invaded China, the world looked the other way. The League of Nations had no teeth because the U.S. Senate had not ratified it. America continued until recently to supply Japan with aviation gasoline and scrap iron, stopping only when she saw she would soon need these things for her own war effort. Why would Germany and Italy not proceed with their conquests, seeing the world's indifference to what happened to China?

Later on, when America began to see the crash coming, her only thought was to make herself safe in the midst of it, like people who participate in a run on a bank. It's too late now for her to be spared the results of her selfishness, but we should all start now working out in our minds what real peace is. We need to be ready for the forces that will again try to impose a vindictive settlement when the war reaches the exhaustion point. In 1919 people were not prepared for the politics of the treaty-makers. This time we must be more aware.

Love to all,

Chapter 24

Letter, Kweiyang, January 6, 1941

Dear Folks,

A while ago I was sitting on the veranda with my feet up, knitting a few rows on the sweater I began during last summer's air raids. I'm not much of a knitter. I should have been taking a nap, but I couldn't deprive myself (or Jeannie, who is in heat and would have had to be shut in with me) of such lovely, warm sunshine.

As I knitted, the amah's *three-year-old daughter stood beside me, as she often does for lack of any better idea of how to play, and chanted to herself everything she could observe about me. You might find her comments interesting.*

"Liu T'ai-t'ai's dress is very long, and so are her pants." (True. They were made in Nanking three years ago when all dresses were long.)

"When Liu T'ai-t'ai sits in a big chair with her feet on a stool you can't see that her tummy is big."

"Liu T'ai-t'ai is striking a hair-thread shirt." (Literal translation for knitting.)"

"When my big sister scolds Bobby she always says 'Shame on oo.'" (The kids have picked up the English expressions we use on the dogs. When this little tyke wants the dogs to go out, she says "Ouch!")

"Liu T'ai-t'ai's dress has a hole burned in the front. One, two, three, four, oh a lot of holes. She had better make a new dress." (Too true, but I hope it will hold out until the end of the pregnancy.)

"The puppy downstairs ate a dirty thing and its tummy swelled up and it died. Liu T'ai-t'ai never eats dirty things, but her tummy swells up, too. When the yellow hen lays an egg Liu T'ai-t'ai eats it right away. Mr. Liu never eats it." (What a pig I sound like! Wally won't eat the few eggs from our hens because he says the baby needs them.)

That should be enough to give you an idea. It's interesting to hear oneself discussed so naively. People on the street talk about me in great detail (especially my big feet) assuming I won't understand.

I used to think the British were the worst for thinking they could discuss foreigners without being understood, but the Chinese are worse. I remember some psychological test in which one question was, "Do you think people are talking about you?" I don't have to think it. I can hear it.

If I should come home for a visit (don't get the idea that I'm about to) Frank and Emily would get a laugh out of my mixture of dialects. They both know pure northern Mandarin. I often don't know what I'm going to call a spoon, or soap, or what-have-you until the word is out because I have so many to choose from. The other day I tried to tell the amah to wash the windows, and she had no idea what I was talking about. At least I don't say "eedeedeederdahger" for "tiny," as she does.

I'm feeling fine now except that I tire easily. All pregnant women do here because of the altitude, well over a thousand meters. I'm still teaching, but the doctor would like me to ease up the second semester. Brother Irving is coming, and will take over my English class as his first step back toward normal work after two years of tuberculosis. That will be good for both of us. I think I can keep on with the French. It would be hard to find a substitute for that.

Love to all,

∾

Peggy arrived in the middle of Saturday afternoon, May 13, 1941, and Wally was there. She howled so that her mouth seemed to be half her face, and he spent a bad night thinking how ugly she was. The next day he said we had better bring her up to be a doctor or something, as no one would marry her. As babies do, she soon assumed human shape, and became the apple of her daddy's eye. She has always kept a jump ahead of me ever since.

Chinese do not celebrate a birth until a month has passed, by which time they can be more confident that the child will survive. On Friday the thirteenth we had a feast for ninety guests in a good restaurant.

By this time I had found a job which I could take as soon as I had adequate household help. In a sprawling old temple three minutes' walk from home were the office and warehouse of an organization calling itself the International Red Cross. (Later the real Red Cross objected to its use of the name, and it became the International Relief Committee, keeping the same initials on its trucks.) They were in desperate need of English-speaking office staff, and would welcome me, baby and all, when I could come to them.

Our amah had left, and we were going through the usual painful process of interviewing possible successors. We settled on Tai Sao, a

Bea and Peggy, Kweiyang, 1941.

dumpy, lumpy little person with great good will and a boundless love for babies. She was physically ugly and a mediocre cook, but she became like one of the family.

Sometime during that long summer, Jeannie brought forth still born puppies and died. No veterinary help was available. This left a gap, which Bobby, her somewhat harebrained son, tried to fill.

I had identical cribs made for home and office, and before Peggy was two months old I began carrying her to the office every day. I had never had anything to do with an office before, but I caught on, and it made me feel as if I were helping the wheels of the world go round.

The Committee had been formed after the disastrous bombing of February 4, 1939, when the whole center of the city had been burned out, taking all drug stores and all hospitals but one. The local foreigners and several influential Chinese pooled all their resources to bring in the help that was needed. The ad hoc effort had matured into a substantial organization with the mission of importing medical supplies for all the civilian hospitals in Free China, and distributing them by truck to wherever they were needed. The government provided only for military hospitals. We also had another function, to receive the remittances from Chinese in Java who wanted to support the war effort, but were not allowed to send money directly to the Chinese government.

The IRC continued to be an interracial venture, having at all times two general managers, one foreign and one Chinese. I am not convinced of the efficiency of having two heads with equal power, but it was a nice idea. The heads at that time were Bill Mitchell of the Canadian Mission and C. T. Miao.

I have never been a professional-quality typist, but I pitched in to catch up on a backlog of correspondence. Then the foreign woman who had volunteered, with more good will than discernment, to do the filing was leaving, and I was asked to create a filing system. The filing had always been done by the light of nature, and was by now thoroughly chaotic. I knew nothing about filing, but I made a plan based on what I knew of library catalogs, and began to redo everything from the beginning. I often found half a dozen topics in one folder, or one topic in half a dozen folders.

A constant problem was keeping track of stock. To bring anything from Hong Kong or Haiphong required a lot of lead time, and we often didn't know something was running low until it was gone. Enter "Uncle Ayres," a retired pharmacist from California who came out "to help

China" without having linked up with any organization. When he got to Hong Kong no one knew what to do with him until he happened to meet our representative who was there buying supplies. He came to our office and became a beloved and colorful part of the effort. He taught us to keep a "perpetual current inventory" so that we knew exactly what we had at any time.

When he left, I was put in charge of the inventory. It was exacting work, and I did it until the office moved to Chungking, shortly before my next child, Sally, was born in November, 1942.

Peggy flourished in the friendly atmosphere of the office, and became a remarkably responsive baby. I was allowed to take time to nurse her and change her diapers as needed.

One day when she was still very small I looked up from my work and saw three young Americans come through the gate. They were John and Irene Vincent and Albert Ravenholt, who had just come, by devious means, across China from the coast. They stayed with us for more than a year, I think. Irene worked in the office with me, John became the coordinator for the shipment of supplies, and Al drove one of our trucks all over Free China, delivering the essentials without which civilian hospitals could not survive.

In the early days of the war in Europe six young Englishmen came to Kweiyang before going on to where they could be useful. Two of them, Owen and Llewellyn Evans, stayed on in our offce for a while, and later joined the Friends' Ambulance Unit (FAU) when it came. Britain at that time recognized the validity of conscientious objection to war, and had special courts to decide on each case. If accepted, the person was given an exemption card but, as these men told us, it was best to get into some kind of humanitarian service somewhere so the neighbors wouldn't feel outraged by seeing them around while others were getting killed. A good, tough job could also allay any suspicion in their own minds that they were cowards.

The Friends' Ambulance Unit shared our office for quite a while until they could set up their own. The head men were Peter Tennant, who became especially fond of Peggy, and Dr. Bob McClure, a China-born missionary who would send out for mid-morning sesame cakes for the staff. Irene and I typed their letters, trying to remember to say "Yours sincerely" instead of "Sincerely yours" to conform to English practice.

Journal, Kweiyang, 1941

It was rather hot even in the shade of the towering pear tree on the south side of the big courtyard, but little Peggy didn't seem to mind. Clad only in a diaper, pinned American style instead of tied, she held the bars of her crib and bounced up and down, keeping up a steady flow of gibberish that sounded just like speech, with commas, periods, and questions, but without any real words in it.

Across the courtyard, in the office of the International Relief Committee, I was busy with a typewriter. Through the gate came a procession of men, each carrying, from a truck outside in the street, two wooden boxes or burlap bales dangling from the ends of a bamboo pole balanced on his shoulder. Some larger cases were hung from a pole carried between two men. The men kept chanting, "Ey-o, ey-o-o" as they took quick, springy steps in time with the chant, so that the heavy weights bobbing at the ends of the poles almost seemed to carry themselves by their rhythmic bouncing.

On the stone platform at the back of the yard, which before the war had been a Confucian temple, white-coated workers, headed by Dr. Helen Mitchell of the Canadian Mission and a Chinese woman pharmacist, were checking the medical supplies as they were brought in. John Vincent was supervising the carriers, who carefully laid down their burdens and went back for more, wiping their sweaty faces with dingy towels as they went.

Peggy shouted with delight as John went over to her crib and held out his fingers for her to swing from. Then he walked quickly across to where I was working.

"Your baby has done the usual thing," he said.

I took a clean diaper and an oilskin bag from my desk drawer and went out to the crib.

At five o'clock John and I took the ends of the crib and carried it through the wide door into the office while Peggy sat in the middle, laughing. Then with the oilskin bag dangling from my wrist, I took her in my arms, watched the gateman lock all the doors opening on the yard, and walked quickly down the cobbled lane to Dragon Spring Street, where our way lay over ancient stone paving between rows of open shops, to the other narrow lane where my own gate was.

As we went, Peggy's bright, brown eyes were never still. Everything was interesting to her.

All along the street people looked up from their work and said to each other, "Here comes the foreign doll." Mothers or grandfathers, standing in doorways with little children in their arms, said, "See the foreign doll!"

The children pointed and repeated, "Foreign doll, foreign doll!"

Children running in the street chanted in unison, "Foreign doll, foreign doll!"

Peggy, too young to be embarrassed, smiled as graciously as any princess, but it was a relief to me when we reached our little lane and I beat with my open hand on the black gate of our house.

"Coming!" shouted Tai Sao, running on her flat feet to open the gate. Her broad, homely face was radiant as she held out her arms for Peggy to jump into. Murmuring a secret language with the baby, she followed me upstairs, along the wide veranda that surrounded the house on three sides, and into the queer, hybrid structure that the builder had concocted under the delusion that he was working in occidental style. Here she set Peggy down in a crib like the one at the office and went to get the eggs that she had dropped into boiling water before she went to open the gate.

I washed Peggy's hands and my own, nursed her briefly, and set her in a little bamboo chair with table attached. Then I broke the eggs into a bowl of mashed potato and gave them to her. She tried to feed herself while I labored to force a cooked carrot through a tea strainer. The meal ended with a drink of the water in which the carrot and some chopped cabbage had been boiled.

Then I took her in my arms and went to the veranda to watch the kites, a kind of large bird, gliding on the evening air currents high in the sky. There Wally found us as he came home from the university. Peggy almost bounced out of my arms in her eagerness to get to him. He spoke English to her, although he was Chinese, because he thought that she was sure to pick up Chinese from the people around her, but might not learn English unless it was the language of the family.

Watching them, I felt well-pleased with my child. Feature for feature she was made in her father's mold, but her skin was fairer and her hair finer than his. We told each other that she was made on his pattern with my materials. I didn't see why people called her a foreign doll.

Yet it was true. When Peggy went on unfamiliar streets with me I heard people say, "The child looks Chinese." When she went with Wally they said, "The child looks like a foreigner." As for Peggy, she was, and always would be, a law unto herself.

◈

One December morning in 1941 I was nursing Peggy and coddling an egg for her on the charcoal fire when someone banged on the gate. Tai Sao opened it and then I heard light footsteps racing along the veranda.

Irene burst into the room and gasped out, "The Japanese bombed Pearl Harbor with fifty planes, and America declared war!" She rushed on with the few details that Bill Mitchell had got from his short-wave radio at four o'clock. He had run to carry the news to the FAU headquarters at Huang T'u P'o, where Irene and John were staying, and Irene had run to me.

I was old enough to remember the First World War, and what America is like when aroused. This, I knew, was just what it would take to make Americans put everything they had into the fight. China had been alone, fighting for life. Now she would not be alone. I said, "Japan has lost the war today."

With dizzying speed, Japan took over Hong Kong, the Philippines, Singapore, and Haiphong. One by one we saw our connections with the outside world severed. There remained only the air route over the "Hump" of the Himalayas, and a still unfinished road to Burma.

The Americans soon decided to set up air bases in Southeast China from which it would be possible to bomb Japan. This was done at enormous expense, flying everything over the Hump, and paying several times the normal price for everything in China. The government maintained an unrealistic exchange rate for transactions with Americans, who had to pay one U.S. dollar for twenty Chinese dollars, when the actual rate for others was several hundred to one.

The Americans agreed to come into China only if they were given complete control of all air traffic. They would not compete for rare cargo space with luxuries for civilians. Nothing could come from India without American permission.

The American Red Cross began to send abundant medical supplies for China, but they were piling up in Calcutta for lack of transport. Our shelves were approaching empty. I remember that the first thing we ran out of was surgical gloves. We were getting letters from hospitals, "If you can't fill this order we will have to close our doors."

We wrote frantic letters to the American top brass wherever they might be: Chungking, Kunming, Calcutta, New Delhi, Washington, begging for a load of Red Cross supplies.

There was a measles epidemic in Kweiyang. Forty children died on one short street near us. To Americans, measles doesn't sound like such a big deal, but in those conditions it ran into fatal pneumonia.

Peggy caught it. I took off work to care for her, going once a day to report her condition to my office chief, who at that time was

Dr. Marian Manly, head of a school of midwifery in Chengtu. She had taken leave of absence to come and help us. When I told her that Peggy seemed to be unconscious most of the time, rousing only enough to cough now and then, she said, "Sulfapyradine."

"And where am I supposed to get any?"

"Don't worry. The first shipment of Red Cross stuff just came in, and we'll get that box out first."

She gave me five precious pills. Gertrude Pao, who was staying with me just then, helped me get it into Peggy. Two pills were enough. By the next morning she was her jolly self again, and I could return three pills to stock.

Owen Evans came to know a French Catholic sister who did what she could for the inmates of the local prisons. He got her to escort a group of us to see the conditions.

We first visited the model prison, where the cells were clean and the food adequate. Gardening and industrial work were required, and the illiterate were taught to read. There was a block of decent private rooms where those with money or influence could live in comfort, with their food cooked by their own servants. We looked into one room with a well-filled bookcase and a large, orderly desk. It belonged to the man who was being punished for failing to assassinate Wang Ching-wei, the arch-puppet of Nanking. This was obviously a place for privileged prisoners, as well as being a showplace.

We went to other places where the best one could say was that they were no worse than prisons everywhere before the days of Elizabeth Fry, the Quaker woman whose work in Newgate Prison started the prison reform movement. They were, in fact, more decent than the one where Joan of Arc was kept, in that men and women were not confined together.

I can never forget the cells holding fifty or more wild-eyed, rawboned men, their scanty rags so impregnated with filth that they could never get any dirtier than they were, their long hair matted into felt, their fingernails curling into broken claws, and their skin rotten with the ulcers of disease and starvation. I could feel their hopeless eyes evaluating my simple clothes and clean, well-nourished body. It was as if my very health were a sign of privilege.

It would be trite to say that they were living like beasts, but it would not be true. No animal but man can live in such degradation. Wild beasts must have a clean, healthy existence or they die. These men would soon die, too, the lucky ones before a firing squad, and the rest by starvation or disease, as only those who had no outside help were in these cells. The sister told us that anyone who had no relatives nearby to send him extra food and bribe his way to a better cell, would die within three months.

In another block of cells, where there were only a dozen men to a room, and they had boards to sleep on, I was startled to hear someone call my name. I saw a small, thin, haggard fellow with what had been a decent cotton suit shapeless from being lived in night and day. I could not remember having seen him before. He looked at me and the hope in his eyes began to fade.

"Liu T'ai-t'ai doesn't remember Old T'ien?"

"Old T'ien!" With this help I could trace in his thin features a resemblance to a fine-looking, intelligent young man who had been a stock boy where I worked. He was the sort who would probably graduate to some minor position of responsibiity.

"Old T'ien! What are you doing here?"

"Liu T'ai-t'ai, I speak speech for you to hear, and beg you to think of a way to help me. You must know that a case of quinine was missing at inventory, and when it was discovered, Old Yao, the gatekeeper, disappeared. When I went to work there, Old Yao was my guarantor, so when he ran away they thought I might have something to do with him, and they put me here."

"That doesn't make sense," I said, "He guaranteed you, you didn't guarantee him. If they didn't want you without a guarantor, they could ask you to get another one, or fire you. They couldn't lock you up for it."

"Whether they could or not, they did. I had only a little money saved, and my wife is already selling our furniture to keep me where I am and give me a little food to eat. I have to pay $2 a day or the guard makes me sleep by the honey bucket. I don't know what my wife and baby are going to eat. I don't ask you to believe me. I only ask you to inquire, and if you find that I have spoken the truth, try to find some influence for me."

Deeply touched, I promised to do my best.

The next day I went to the man in charge to check up on the story, which proved to be true. I protested against making him suffer for another man's fault. The manager, who prided himself on his administrative ability but never thought of himself as cruel, waved his hand airily as he said, "How could I run this place if I let goods disappear and didn't punish anyone for it?"

"Well, you'd think differently if you could see the place where he is. He's so starved already that I could scarcely recognize him."

He reached for the telephone and withdrew his complaint against Old T'ien. The next day the poor fellow was back at work, which was more than I had dared hope for. He never again became the bright, ambitious lad he had been. Months later he was still thin, and I heard that he was spitting blood, an indication of tuberculosis. He didn't seem concerned about the blood, but he wanted to get some cough medicine for his child.

Twice we received large shipments of clothes and other necessities from the Lord Mayor's Fund in London. Many of these things were useful, but some were almost laughably unsuitable. Large quantities of good woolen yarn had been knitted by charitable English ladies into baby afghans or sweaters. Wool was not used in Chinese clothing except by the more prosperous classes who had been influenced by foreign ideas. If we had given these woolens to refugees they would not have known how to wash them without shrinking, nor would they have had suitable soap for the purpose.

Although we had some qualms about selling relief supplies, we thought it better to sell those materials at a low price to those who could use them, and use the money to buy useful things. Many Chinese women were good knitters, but they did not wrap babies in wool. They ripped up the afghans and sweaters and reknitted them in a suitable size.

Some old, retired missionary lady (I'm sure) watched over the cutting and sewing of Chinese children's clothes of fine English materials in the fashion of more than fifty years earlier. No use could be found for those. I was thankful to be allowed to buy some clothing for Peggy, and also a memorable rag doll with a white face on one end and a black one on the other, with a reversible skirt.

Chapter 25

There were changes in our lives with the new war situation. Japan was much too busy extending her hold on Southeast Asia to think of bombing Kweiyang. We had a lovely, peaceful spring and summer. I had supposed that I might always duck if I heard heavy airplanes, but I got so used to hearing American planes going about their business that I got over that reflex.

(Or thought I did. In 1945, in Calcutta, I was just sitting down to breakfast when I suddenly thought, "Those bombers are right overhead," and I got under the table, to the amazement of my tablemates.)

I continued to work at the IRC. American Quakers were coming to join the FAU. The American law was less clear than that of England about conscientious objection, but it was still possible for some young men to convince their draft boards of their sincere opposition to war.

I became concerned about having Peggy confined to her crib all the time. It was not feasible to have her crawling around the floor at the office, even if it had been clean enough. The floor at home was definitely not clean enough, and was splintery besides, so I put on a campaign to get it well scrubbed. This had to be done with care lest the water go through the cracks onto the family below. Then I spread a blanket down and gave Peggy her first taste of freedom. She didn't know what to do with it at first, but was soon crawling as if she had done it all her life.

For some reason the IRC decided to move to Chungking. I stuck with them until the end, but was not sorry to see them go. I was pregnant again, and was busy preparing for a move to Hua-ch'i, a famous scenic spot thirteen miles away, where new buildings had been built for the university.

Great China University (Ta Hsia) would become National Kweichow University, a government institution.

Since Sally was due in November, it seemed best for Wally to go first, leaving Tai Sao and Peggy and me within reach of the hospital. He had to be away three days a week.

During one of my routine prenatal examinations, young Dr. Hsu suddenly became alert and asked another doctor to verify her finding.

The fetus was now big enough so they could tell the head from the tail, and know that the head was where the tail should be. They worked over me, but could not correct the problem. They told me to rest with my hips elevated for two days and then come back. Still no luck, so they told me I would have to expect a breech delivery.

When I told Marian Manly, who was head of a school of midwifery, she said she had a trick which she taught to her midwives, and she would try it on me if I wished. She wouldn't do it until the eighth month, as it might just possibly induce premature labor. At the proper time she came to my house. She found the head and bent it forward, which made Sally uncomfortable so she gave a big kick and flipped around. Marian rolled up two bath towels and bound them against my tummy to try to hold the position. At the next examination Dr. Hsu was overjoyed to find the position correct. I confessed what we had done, and Marian had some very interested pupils at the maternity hospital.

The last few nights before Sally was born I slept at the hospital so as not to risk having to argue my way through the city gate at night. The sixteen bed ward was nearly empty, and the staff were sitting around the stove making dressings or baby clothes.

One evening on my way over I sprained my ankle, so I didn't want to go home the next day. Rather than keep me waiting in that condition, they gave me quinine and castor oil to hurry things along. For hours I had very weak pains and made little progress. They said that when the pains got strong I could go to the delivery room, which I did. As I lay reading, a midwife sat near by making dressings.

I asked to be examined. She said, "At the rate you're going it will be another couple of hours."

I thought, "Like fun I'll feel like this for two hours, but I'll wait twenty minutes before asking again." Before the twenty minutes were up the water broke. The doctor rushed in and began to wash her hands. Before she was done somebody was holding the head back with a sterile towel.

By the time I came out of the first delivery room, the other one was occupied, and someone was waiting for mine. Both rooms were constantly in use from then on. The hospital that had been empty became a beehive. Through the night more women kept coming, in various stages of urgency. They were examined as they came in. If there was time they were sent to another hospital, or with a crew for home delivery, but if they were too advanced they had to be taken in somehow. All sixteen beds were full, and doors were being laid on trestles to make more beds, with bedding brought from the patient's home. At five a.m. I heard someone say, "What are we going to do? We're running out of sterile dressings." Someone was sent in a rickshaw to borrow from another hospital.

Sally was a good-natured baby, but I had scarcely time to get acquainted with her before disaster struck. She was born November 21st. Soon after we got home I began feeling not quite well. I supposed it was just post-partum stress and would pass.

Early on Christmas morning, before Wally got back from Hua-ch'i, I felt uneasy enough so that I decided to go quickly and see Dr. Hsu before she might get away. She listened to me at the door and said I couldn't come into the maternity hospital because it might be something contagious. With such an insidious onset, it might be typhoid fever. I must go at once to the Central Hospital, taking Sally with me, and she would telephone them to be expecting me.

I went home, gathered up a few things and the baby, gave Tai Sao instructions about Peggy, and set out alone in a rickshaw for the Central Hospital on the other side of the city. Someone was waiting for me at the door, and what followed is best told in the poem which I wrote later:

TYPHUS AT CHRISTMAS

It was not a bed, it was a furnace,
And I the firepot.
They had taken my baby from me when I came
Alone in a rickshaw across the city,
And I did not know where she was.
I had to believe they knew what they were doing,
The vague forms that came and went,
Doctors and nurses.
Sometimes I caught words:
"The fever is awfully high."
"Could be typhus but I'm guessing typhoid."

Fire around me, in me;
I had to keep stoking the fire,
Find something of me to feed it with.
Typhus—

Don't know anything about it
Except that people die of it
In wars and disasters.
Something about rats? lice? fleas?
Typhoid, from dirty food or water,
Long and dangerous.
But I have to live!
I have a new baby.
She needs my milk and my love.
I'm too tired to think,
But just remember that one thing:
Sally needs me.

"Can you take a little tea?
I'll hold your head up. . . ."
"Try some eggnog. . . ."
I do try to do what they ask,
To keep my head clear long enough to swallow,
But trying brings on a coughing spell.
Leave me alone! Leave me alone!
But Sally needs me.
I must try.

My head is working better.
I ask the doctor,
"Is it typhus?"
"I'm not sure yet," he says,
"Typhus will last two weeks.
Typhoid takes longer.
Either way you are going to win.
You are a strong girl
And you have babies who need you."
I'm glad he didn't use double talk.
It's a game with death,
And Sally and I are going to win.

I call the nurse.
"Bring the baby to me.
I must feed her to keep my milk."

"I will ask the doctor," she says.
Sally is brought
To lie beside me briefly
Before her bottle.
She doesn't get much,
One side only . . .
It's too hard to turn over.

Tears, what's the sense of tears
Rolling down onto the pillow?
Sally had a rash,
And she sucked so little!
But we are going to win,
She and I.
I hate wet pillows:
Sweat, tears, it's wet so often.

I can chew now,
But the soft rice and pickles
Are hard to get down.
I do try.
I must eat to make milk;
I must eat for Sally.
I tell myself,
This is all they can afford,
There are so many sick.

But a nurse comes in
With a fresh loaf of bread,
Warm and fragrant.
Where did it come from?
She says, "The hospital matron
Knows how to bake bread.
She thought you might like it.
We'll keep it here,
And you can have a slice
Whenever you like."

She cuts the crisp crust
And spreads it with the lard

She keeps for my dry lips.
It is good.
I drift to sleep
With a warm feeling:
I'm not alone.
They really care about me.

To sleep . . . to dream:
I am a child of five
In my mother's kitchen.
The breeze blows the curtains
And brings in the fragrance of the lilacs.
Mother opens the oven
And takes out six golden loaves
More fragrant than the breeze.
I can't wait.
She cuts a crisp crust
And spreads it with butter.
If one must be sick
It is good to pass the time
Having such dreams.

When I wake it is no longer
Just Sally and I against death,
It is a crowd:
Husband and child at home,
Father and Mother half a world away,
The doctors and nurses,
And a woman I have never seen
Who cares enough to bake me bread.
And death has slunk away, overwhelmed.

I call for a slice of bread,
And now she has made marmalade for it.

There was a lot of typhus in Kweiyang at that time. It was the fleaborne, not the louseborne kind, but even so a serious matter. There was no way to prevent a flea from jumping on you in a rickshaw.

Sally was not kept in the nursery for fear of infection, but was in a crib in my unheated room except at feeding time. She was remarkably patient as she lay wet and neglected. The nursing school was having the same problem I had had in teaching. The wartime standards in the middle schools were so low that students were not prepared to cope with what came next. The half-trained student nurses were incredibly inept. Sally rarely had any care except at meal time.

Six nurses excellently trained in Hong Kong had come to Kweiyang to wait for their certification exams to come from England, as they could not get them in Japanese-held Hong Kong. They were helping out at Central Hospital. Twice in three weeks one of them came on her own time, built a charcoal fire in the room, and gave Sally a bath.

My fever broke in two weeks, and in a few days more I could go home. They said I must give Sally a bottle because my milk wouldn't be enough. With milk powder at $20,000 a pound, this was no laughing matter. I soon noticed that she wasn't taking all the milk I had. She had got used to having it come easily from a bottle. I fed her every time she wanted it, even if it was only fifteen minutes since the last, but tried to get her to take all I had. Within three days she was back on a four-hour schedule, getting plenty.

Her skin, when I took her home, was like raw beef, but with regular care it soon recovered.

After this experience of abandonment, it took her a long time to learn to trust life.

Chapter 26

In March we moved to Hua-ch'i, where we shared a supposedly foreign-style house with three other families. We had three rooms upstairs and a kitchen downstairs. Our windows looked out over a rice field to a double row of old trees with a path between. The path turned and ran past a small hill, and on into the mountains. Another path, behind our house, crossed the rice field. I loved to take the children to play on the hill.

We took on a manservant, Chiang Shih, who went to market, carried water, and did many other chores, so that Tai Sao had more time for the children. Chiang Shih lost no time in seducing the neighbor's *amah*, whose husband worked in Kweiyang. As soon as she suspected that she was pregnant she went to visit her husband, so when the bundle of joy arrived he came out with a fat chicken to celebrate. Everyone kept a straight face.

I made a garden in an open space by the house, but I didn't know that a garden had to be fenced. The domestic animals, from chickens and piglets to horses and water buffalo, roamed freely and did not scruple to graze my garden clean.

By this time I knew that Tai Sao had a wonderful way with children. She was more alert than I to things that might hurt them. She had done well with Peggy when I was sick. I need have no qualms about leaving both chldren with her when I went back to teaching.

I would never have thought of teaching tricks to a little baby, but Tai Sao had no problem with it. At six months Sally could imitate a dog, a cat, a rooster, a buffalo and a pig, and could pretend to go to sleep.

All kinds of people loved Tai Sao. When we left Kweiyang the Confucian scholar's family downstairs invited her to stay with them whenever she came to town to see her mother. At the old scholar's funeral she was asked to be the comforter, the one who tells the mourners they have keened long enough.

She lost no time in making friends among our Miao tribal neighbors. When they had trouble they would come to her, and if the problem was beyond her she would come to me.

"Miao Ima's niece had a baby last night in a house with no fire, and they've nothing to wrap it in."

I bustled around and found what we could spare of our own scanty possessions.

"Miao Ima's baby won't eat. Can you look at it?"

Miao Ima was a hopeless slattern married to an old widower who had only daughters by his first marriage. No woman worth her salt would marry him, and he would put up with anything to get a son. I had tried to get them to use the new provincial hospital for the birth, but the tribespeople wanted no part of modern medicine.

The baby was a fine, strong boy who could hold his head up at birth, but now, after six days, he was in trouble. I went to see him, knowing what I would find. The local name for tetanus was "seven day fits" because if the cord is cut with a dirty instrument it takes that long for the infection to travel up the cord and kill. Most babies died this way.

I found that the child had not wetted a diaper for two days, but they hadn't worried about that. It just meant that he was a good baby, no trouble. Now he wouldn't eat. Could I help?"

I watched and saw a repeated twitching of the lips, a sure sign of tetanus. "I'm sorry," I said, "Nothing can be done for this baby. Next time you must go to the hospital. They don't let the seven day fits get into a baby."

I found out that the tribal custom prescribed breaking a new bowl and using the freshly broken edge to cut the cord, a fairly sanitary procedure. The father, unable or unwilling to afford a new bowl, had picked up a shard from the ground. I told Tai Sao to keep promoting the idea of going to the hospital next time.

"She says there won't be a next time. She has had five and lost them all the same way, and she's tired of it. She won't do it again."

"How can she keep from having another?"

"She will go out on the mountain and find a certain plant that will keep her from having children."

So maybe that poor old father will never have a son, but he has three fine, capable daughters from his first marriage. One of them was my neighbor, Pao Mei.

Journal, Hua-ch'i, 1943

I'm glad I have seen Pao Mei's house. She is as perfect a housekeeper as I have ever seen anywhere. It would have been too bad for me to carry away the memory of Miao Ima's house as typical of tribal living.

I know now that all Miao Ima's relatives regard her with contempt. She spreads the bed on the dirt floor, separated only by a two-foot bank from the buffalo. She never seems to sun, air, mend or wash anything.

Pao Mei is one of her stepdaughters. She usually wears a simple blouse and pants for working, saving her elaborate tribal costume, spun, dyed, woven and embroidered by her own hands, for festivals. She will do anything that will bring in an honest dollar. She was the one who carried great loads of sticks from the mountain to fence my garden. She has said that if we can ever get rid of our manservant she would like to do our heavy work to learn our ways.

Her house is one room, a framework of poles lashed together and well thatched, with a thin screen of straw for walls, but they have somehow acquired good, substantial furniture, fit for the better house they hope to build. Everything is shiny clean. Even the corner with the brick stove is clean, and the twigs for starting the fire are piled so neatly that they are almost an ornament. The dirt floor is carefully swept. In one corner I saw a bamboo cage with two resplendent pheasants pecking at steamed grain to fatten them for market. The buffalo and the brood sow with her piglets are sheltered outside the house.

Pao Mei didn't know I was going to see her, so I know she hadn't tidied up for me.

She brings me gifts of delicious tribal food whenever I show her any small courtesy. The best I could do for her was some of the steamed bakingpowder bread I invented and the crazy marmalade I make of carrots and tangerine skins.

Today I had a chance to do something for her. She had one housekeeping problem she hadn't solved. When she hung a piece of pork over the stove to smoke, rats ran down the rope. I got the lid of a dry milk tin to make a disk on the rope, as they do on ships' hawsers. I hope it works.

I feel inferior to Pao Mei. What would she not have made of my opportunities?

∾

I had the remainder of that year to rest, but had to teach the following year.

One winter day I went home and found a dumpling-wrapping party in progress. The room seemed very cold. I pulled the brazier out from under the table and added charcoal, fanning it to get a brighter glow. I couldn't get the place warm enough.

Someone asked, "Are you trying to cook us for dinner?"

"It's cold in here. Don't you think so?"

A survey showed a consensus that it was very hot.

"Maybe you have malaria," said one.

"How would I get malaria in winter?"

"If you've ever had it, you still have it. It can hit you any time. Take quinine if you have any, and go to bed."

Wally found the quinine left over from that occasion, but I waved it away. I was thinking I might be pregnant, and quinine could spoil it. I asked him to try to get Atebrin instead, the new drug which was hard to get because it was saved for the military. The guests scattered to track down rumors of Atebrin, but without success.

I went to bed and piled on all our covers and warm gowns, and shivered until, in its own good time, fever crept into me, turning my body into a raging furnace.

Wally came back empty-handed, and gathered up our supply of towels for when the fever would break. He gave me lots of cool boiled water, and took care of the baby.

At last, after an eternity in Hell, I began to sweat.

Wally wrapped me in bath towels and changed them when they were wet. My temperature returned to normal, and I slept.

During my day of remission, Wally continued his search for Atebrin. I was still unwilling to risk my pregnancy by taking quinine. My second attack, coming punctually forty-eight hours after the first, was more violent, and the third even worse. I thought the chill would shake my teeth loose, and the fever seemed to be consuming my substance. Even on the days of remission, I felt more and more depleted.

On hearing that there was Atebrin at Yale-in-China medical college, Wally took the shaky old bus (faster than a pony cart) to Kweiyang. He expected to be back in time to head off a fourth attack. I waited . . . and waited. . . . The hands of my watch moved inexorably toward the hour for the attack.

At last I thought, "I'm not sure there's a baby, and if there is it must have been damaged by the fever." I took a stiff dose of quinine, and fifteen minutes later Wally came in with the Atebrin.

It was a long, slow road back to full health. Getting out of bed I might feel my heart churning and pounding so that I had to hang on to Sally's crib for a while. Walking to school I often had to hug a tree until my heart settled down. A young doctor at the hospital assured me that my heart was normal, but I didn't believe it. I went again on the day when the director would be there. He said I was anemic. "There's a Chinese saying that one attack of malaria costs four ounces of blood," he said. "I can't test your blood because my hemometer is broken, but you can see for yourself that your fingernails are blue."

I had a sickening flashback to the blue fingernails that warned me of my first baby's mortal illness.

"Could that make my heart act so funny?"

"Yes. We'll fix up your blood and you'll be all right."

And so it proved, except that the following summer there was an even worse assault on my blood.

In the meantime, as spring came on, I was determined to build such a fence that it would be safe to plant a garden. It was forbidden to cut anything nearby, because of a feeble effort at reforestation. I hired tribespeople to bring backloads of thorn branches from far out in the hills, and also to cut such willow branches as they could. We set these in the ground to enclose a fairly large space, with willow branches at frequent intervals. These we kept watered, and they put forth roots, anchoring the fence. We took twenty-foot canes of a kind of climbing wild rose to weave into the fence for stability.

My neighbor, Auntie Sheng, in whose house I had stored things before we moved to Hua-ch'i, became my gardening mentor, providing me with seeds and telling me the local methods. She gave me lots of seeds of a kind of marigold which grew thick and tall. I planted them all around the outside of the fence. A kind of climbing bean on the inside made the fence so tight that only one tiny piglet ever got through.

I loved preparing the soil with the only tool available, similar to a grub-hoe, and planting a great variety of vegetables with seeds provided by Auntie Sheng. I had red and yellow tomatoes in several shapes and sizes, and green vegetables and root vegetables in abundance. There were also peanuts, sweet potatoes and something that I called pumpkin, but other people, under English influence, called marrow. I took pleasure in providing not only our own table but those of friends. Sometimes our male helper took a load to market to barter for other things we needed.

But during the summer I had another threatened miscarriage. I had no Dr. Li handy with sandbags, but I was serious about lying still. The local doctor gave me bromides to relax me, but I bled and bled. Time after time it seemed as if I might try to sit up, but each time there was another mass of clots and I had to lie still again.

At last the doctor said that this was beyond her competence, and I must go to a specialist in Kweiyang. Wally somehow wangled a car to take me to the Central Hospital. Verdict: I had aborted long before, but incompletely. I must have a D. & C. to clear out the remnants. This was done, with magical effect, and a day or so later I was turned loose to find my way home. After such a long time in bed, I was indescribably weak, and felt as if I had been beaten all over with clubs, but I managed to find the bus depot and get home. With good food and iron pills I recovered rapidly and was soon back in the garden.

I remember hearing a neighbor say, "That Liu T'ai-t'ai is something else. She has read books, but she can still dig the earth."

∾

I had heard that the landlord-tenant relationship in China resembled the feudal system in medieval Europe, but I had only one chance to see it in action.

One of our colleagues who had come from Shanghai with the university, happened to be the owner of a considerable area two days' walk over the mountains from where we were. From years as an absentee landlord, he suddenly became a feudal lord with a personal relationship to his tenants.

Twice a year the tenants made a two-day trek, carrying on shoulder poles his share of the harvest, enough to make him rich by our standards. He built a fine house in Western style, with a large walled garden, the showplace of the village.

He had some reciprocal reponsibilities, such as protecting the young men from conscription. Two of them were working as servants in his home for this reason. When the army press gangs became more aggressive, a younger boy came demanding protection. The landlords didn't want another mouth to feed, so they gave the boy, P'en Ch'i-ts'ai, to me to carry water and work in the garden. I was to give his wages to them, not to him.

It was bitterly cold when P'en Ch'i-t'sai came to us. We asked him whether he had a warm quilt, and he said yes. He slept in the kitchen, and the next day he was limping. His foot was hard and red. I saw his quilt, which was a pitiful old rag, not big enough to cover him. At the district hospital, he was put to bed with gas gangrene from frostbite in the foot. We spent the equivalent of two months' wages on him before he was fit to work.

For his homecoming we provided a warm quilt and a padded suit, second-hand but sound. He ate with Tai Sao, flavoring his abundant rice with left-overs from our table. He was cheerful and willing, and found many ways to be helpful.

After a few days the landlord's wife came to see me, her face like a thundercloud. "You've got to quit spoiling that boy or I'll take him back."

"How am I spoiling him?"

"Giving him new things and fancy food, and sending him to the hospital. He comes over and brags to my servants about his clothes and the good food he gets. It makes my servants discontented. I can't afford to treat them that way. If you don't quit showering him I'll send him back to the farm. If he gets conscripted it's just too bad."

"I don't feel that we've given him anything but basic necessities," I said, "but I'll tell him not to show off to your servants anymore. I think, however, that you cannot properly take him back until he has worked long enough to cover his hospital bills. I will retain his wages until that is paid off."

I never did turn his wages over to her, but kept them to give to him in a lump when he left us.

ॐ

Student volunteers for service as interpreters with the American army came before me for testing in spoken English.

"Why do you wish to leave school and take up this work?"

Over and over came the stiff reply, "I think it is my duty to serve my country."

Now and then I met a more human frankness. "It is hard for my father to keep so many children in school in these times. The Americans pay well, so I can relieve his burden and have enough to help the others."

A thin, large-eyed boy came in. His words came rather slowly, a little below standard. His eyes glistened with tears as he said, "I have to fight the Japanese, but I am too weak to fire a gun. The only weapon I can offer is my English. I must go. I hate war. My home was in Changteh . . ."

His tears spilled over as I remembered what I had heard of Changteh at the time of its recapture after some of the fiercest fighting of the war. Not a roof was left in the city, and the earth was scorched for miles around.

"My home was wiped out. My old parents had to run away. If they were alive they would have written. If you will let me go I will work twice as hard as the others."

I weighed his frail body and halting speech against his earnest spirit. An incompetent interpreter might cost many lives, but he would have three months' training before final acceptance. I passed him.

Chapter 27

As the inflation progressed, it became impossible to live on a set salary. Any amount agreed upon at the beginning of a contract soon became ridiculous. The first solution was to peg the salary to the price of rice, so that it rose automatically with the cost of living. This was fine until the money spoiled so fast that it wasn't good from one payday to the next. Then we were paid in actual rice, an occasional handout of cotton cloth or lamp oil, and a small amount in crisp, new banknotes. The rice ensured our basic nourishment, and could be sold little by little during the month to provide for other needs.

Since the rice was supposed to ensure subsistence, the allowance for a college president or a janitor was the same. There was a decree that if husband and wife both worked they would get only one rice allowance. The working wives went on strike, saying they weren't crazy enough to work for money. We got our rice.

I found that the country people, seeing that professors always used fresh banknotes, supposed that people of our class could print their own money.

Even with two rice allowances, we found it impossible to meet our obligations. Tubercular brother Irving was dependent on us, and Wally's parents, cut off from their source of income, needed help. Wally took a desperate measure to cope with the inflation. Every teacher needed some kind of extra income. The most lucrative of all was to buy an old truck, hire a driver and mechanic, and go into the hauling-plus-profiteering business. I will never understand how Wally scraped up the capital to do this. On school vacations he went himself on the truck, hauling a contract cargo and also buying things where they were cheap and selling them where they were scarce. When he could not go along himself, the harelipped driver, Ho-ho, was well able to manage. Like the few other trucks still limping along in Free China, the old clunk was under repair more days than it was on the road, but the mechanic's boundless ingenuity kept it running, and it eased our economic crunch substantially.

I wanted a goat as the only way to get milk for the children. Chinese goats are not bred for milking, as milk has never been part of the Chinese diet, but I could at least get a pint or so. Goats would be in the market in the spring.

One winter day Wally saw a man leading a goat to market. He brought him to the house and asked whether I wanted it. It was a well-formed brown nanny, just weaning a white billy. She would give milk right away. I took her.

I had never milked, and she had never been milked. I had Chiang Shih get her against the wall and sit on her while I washed her and tried to master the new skill.

The next morning I noticed that she limped. She had a badly in-fected foot where a thorn had festered. That must have been why she was sold out of season. It was a long struggle to clear up the infection. Nanny took a lot of my time for several months, and rewarded me with a small but precious amount of milk. Many people think goat milk is smelly, but this is true only if the goat is not well washed. The milk from a clean goat is delicious.

∾

After a gap during which letters did not reach home and I did not keep a journal, there is a scrappy sort of diary covering parts of 1943 and 1944. A few quotations may give the flavor of that period.

"Peggy wakened in distress at four and hasn't slept again. Sally learned to pull herself to her feet yesterday, and now she's too busy to sleep. Last night at nine she was still standing up. I could use a nap . . .

"One of my major problems is to get rid of junk. I can't toss it because it is not mine alone. Also, things that would normally be classed as junk must be kept because they are irreplaceable. More than once I have pulled out some discarded item and put it back into service because it was better than what I was using . . .

"Lately I have been thinking of writing short things instead of the book I have had in mind so long. I must use all the time I can find to experiment with suitable forms . . .

"It would be nice to be able to teach a love of literature instead of just struggling to overcome language deficiency. The courses laid out by the Ministry of Education presume that the basics have been learned in middle school, but in fact nobody with a good command of English is teaching in middle school now, and my students have to be taught basic sentence structure. Sometimes

they say, 'We did that in middle school. Now we want to read Shakespeare,' but they can no more read Shakespeare than I can read Homer, which is to say they might be able to puzzle out a few lines a day, but never get the feel of it. They have been taught to write down every new word in a notebook. They write down long lists of words every day, including the same ones over and over, because no one can learn so many. I tell them to choose ten words a day to learn and let the rest go, but they don't do it . . .

"The University received an allotment of cotton cloth to be divided among the faculty. When Wally went to get it he was told I already had mine. My name had been marked off. I suppose I must go and make a fuss. I hate to, but whoever is doing that sort of thing should be stopped. It is probable that we are all getting cheated in various ways, and I must make an issue of it . . .

"I did get my cloth, and found out (most interestingly) who was the villain. Now I know why I never liked him . . .

"Teaching is bad for me, as anything is that one doesn't do well. I am not effective in front of a group of people who don't understand me, but won't admit it . . .

"The book about the war years needs to be done while people are still interested in the subject. Americans have a short attention span. Meantime I try to find time to work on my little story . . .

"I think I should refuse to renew my contract, and live by selling things while I work on my book. We have lots of stuff which is rare and costly now but will be of no value once the war is over, and the end is definitely in sight. Wally's sense of security is somehow bound up with my teaching. Any writing other than straight journalism such as he was taught in college seems frivolous to him . . .

"That poor, insane beggar woman is sitting on the ground under my window scratching herself. It makes me rage to think that there is no way to help such a person . . .

"I'm satisfied with my decision not to teach. I hope Wally will accept it. He's away on a truck trip now and I'm afraid he will balk at the idea of selling things. I wish I had someone other than Wally to give me an opinion on my writing . . .

"It's up to me to simplify and organize our living, even if I have to spend some money to do it. I must have a desk of my own, or at least some clear space used by no one else to keep notes and manuscripts not only private but accessible. I thought I got my own desk last year. I put it in the darkest corner so Wally wouldn't use it, but of course when we heated only one room in winter . . .

"Wally came home all steamed up to sell all our junk quick and buy U.S. dollars, which he has found a way to get at 190-1. I agree in principle, but I'm afraid the implication is that I should teach, so we won't have to spend money of stable value . . .

"Once in bed I couldn't relax. For hours I struggled to make peace with the idea of teaching, saying goodbye to the brain babies that have been taking shape in my mind. I can't make myself accept it. Am I a jellyfish? . . .

"Wally found the story I was working on and read it, and said, 'Why do you want to write this sort of stuff?' Suddenly I lost my taste for it. Why is there no one I can turn to for reassurance that anyone would want to read what I write? . . .

"Wally's going to sell the truck as soon as it earns another tire. A truck sells for the value of its tires, and it's allowed a new one at the official rate (20 to 1) every so many miles. In selling the truck the tire will count at its black market rate, which will make it a very profitable deal. It's crazy arithmetic, like everything we do . . .

"I had a terrible dream last night. I was carrying Sally when I fell into a quagmire. I pulled myself out, but she was still lying on the surface. I knew if I went back for her we'd both be lost. I had an awful time trying to find boards to approach her with. The only hope seemed to be the thin boards from somebody's bed, but they kept splitting. I could never get to the point of pulling her out. The dream kept shying away from that climax, while my mind remained full of agonized effort. I wakened to chase a rat, and couldn't sleep again for a long time. Every time I dozed off a little I saw her lying there half submerged in the mire, and I had a sense of desperation lest she sink before I could get to her. I had to waken myself and apply the treatment I taught Peggy the other night when she was afraid of beggars in a dream. I said over and over, 'There is no mud here. Sally is sleeping in her bed.' Then I made myself think of other things . . .

"I heard that there will be an American hospital for wounded aviators in Hua-ch'i. That might be a good place to work. I must find out quick, as it's not fair to keep the university dangling . . . Tai Sao's hemorrhoids bled again, so she's white and weak. She didn't tell me until last night. I must get money from the bank and send her to the doctor today . . .

"The die is cast. I signed my teaching contract yesterday. I'll have one French and one English. I must go this morning and get my salary, as Wally

has left on the truck, and I spent all my money for coal yesterday. I must try to find a book for English exercises, or I'll have to write one."

Journal, Hua-ch'i, September 24, 1944

The landlord's wife came to say they want us out of the house in three weeks. Government and business offices in Kweiyang are trying to get their people out of the city as the war comes close, and the Central Bank wants our house.

I went to school to ask about the house situation, and they said to sit tight. Chinese custom requires three months' notice to evict a tenant. I'm to say it's the school's business, not mine, as they rented the house, and I will move as soon as they find me a place. They will stall for the full three months.

I had meant to go to Kweiyang next Monday for my glasses, but instead I went right out and hailed a passing Jeep. There were four American officers in it, including Colonel Powell of the Medical Corps and a man who used to be in the forestry station at Cass Lake. They said the Army will evacuate me in case of need, and Wally too. If the Japanese advance with little or no resistance they can't average more than ten miles a day, and at that rate we have two months' grace. They hope the war in Europe will be over by then amd the Allies will get out here in force before all the good bases in China are gone. Colonel Powell hadn't known that there is typhus in Kweiyang.

It was in Kweiyang that I began to take seriously the rumor that we might have to evacuate. I don't have to worry about how we'd get away, as the Army would take us all. I have been making a list of things that must be ready if any hasty departure is to be anything but chaos:

Preparations to Make in Case:
1. Get my passport visaed (it lapsed a year ago),
2. Have winter clothes for kids, and sound clothes for all,
3. Plan what to do with things we would leave,
4. Pack essential documents, compact valuables, address book, etc. in form we can take if we can't take much.
5. See if Wally can get American passport.

Journal, Hua-ch'i, October 4, 1944

I went to Kweiyang twice and had new glasses made, fountain pen repaired, etc. Cost of glasses, $5,000. They make a wonderful difference. I hadn't had new ones for nine years, and my vision was getting pretty poor.

We may not be able to stay here much longer. The Central Bank demands our house. The Americans are being kicked out of their air bases. The war is coming close to us at last . . .

That's the end of the diary. The last page of the notebook is cramped notes in tiny writing. What follows is a coherent account of the contents of these notes.

Chapter 28

After a long respite while the action was on other fronts, our war came back to life. The Japanese pushed down through Hunan and Kwangsi, forcing the evacuation of the enormously costly American air bases, built and supplied by flights over the "Hump" of the Himalayas, which had been planned to provide a way to attack Japan. These bases had never been protected by ground forces because Chiang Kai-shek deemed it unnecessary. He thought air power was invincible. Now the Americans were in flight (as described in Theodore White's *The Mountain Road*), blowing up bases and supplies, and demolishing bridges as soon as their own forces were over, without regard to the fleeing civilians behind.

Kweiyang was jittery. Government offices and important businesses were trying to move to safe places in the country. Hua-ch'i (Flowery River), where we lived, was eminently desirable, being only thirteen miles out, but on a side road, away from the main advance.

We and three other families occupied one of the few even moderately "foreign style" houses in Hua-ch'i. Not surprisingly, the Central Bank decided that it must have that house for its employees. We stalled as long as we could, but on September 25th came the notice that we must be out in three weeks. We had, of course, been scouting out alternatives. The best was a Chinese style house just across the road, with a paved courtyard and wooden floors. We could have two small rooms plus space in the hallway for cooking and Tai Sao. There was a place to stack the large supply of charcoal we had laid in for winter. It was far from adequate, but it would have to do. Most of the village was thatched cottages with tamped earth floors.

With Tai Sao's help we set to work. We scrubbed the floor, built shelves and papered the walls. White wallpaper is the rule, not merely for cosmetic effect, but to seal cracks where bugs might breed. Professional papering was prohibitive, but we had a way. For a long time I had been receiving a newsletter for Americans (put out by the Consulate? the Information Service?) which was printed on one side of heavy white paper such as was never seen otherwise. I had a huge stack of these saved up, and Wally laboriously pasted them all over our walls. The effect was stunning.

On November 13th I went to class as usual in the morning. After lunch the men came to move us. The distance was short but the confusion great. In the midst of it there was an air raid alarm, but we were far enough from the city not to let it keep us from our task. By the next day, moving was almost complete and I had a big organizing job to do.

On the 17th I had to go to class. There I learned that the university was going to be evacuated to Hsuyang, a village in the mountains, and Wally was to be in charge of the move. His outstanding initiative, plus the fact that he owned two trucks, made him the obvious choice for the job. We decided that this must be the time for me to take the children and make a visit home to America. Mother had died recently, and Dad had begged me to come.

I finished the moving by flashlight. Then, out of the blue, came my brother-in-law, Shou-yu, Emily's husband, with my steamer trunk which he had somehow managed to bring all the way across China from Tientsin, through guerrilla country and the Japanese lines. What a treasure it would have been earlier—two winter coats and lots of other things that I needed! Now it was just a lot more things that I could sell in Chungking to get foreign exchange for my trip.

The joyous reunion with Shou-yu was marred by the urgencies of the moment. He pitched in to help, and made himself very popular with the children. Peggy still remembers the night of the full moon, when he took them to the paved yard and drew around their shadows with chalk.

On November 18th I took a pony cart (we called them horse carriages) to the American Army headquarters at the Kweiyang race track to look for a Captain Smith, who was said to be the person to see about possible evacuation. No luck. There was an alarm but they paid no attention. I was on my way to Erh Ch'iao (Second Bridge) to see Captain Barnes when the urgent alarm came, so I was not allowed to keep walking on the main road. I sat in a cemetery for a while and then headed across fields toward Erh Ch'iao. I turned out to be on the wrong side of the river, so I had to go back and get a horse carriage.

Captain Barnes was very nice. He promised all possible help, and said that Wally or Tai Sao or both could go with me. He gave me a lift back to town in a Jeep. I spent the night at the China Inland Mission.

Back in Hua-ch'i, I kept working on preparations to leave. I met my classes only sporadically. On November 28th I talked with some officers and Arthur Lin, who came by in a Jeep. They said the Japanese could be expected in Kweiyang in about six days. They were already near Tushan, only sixty miles away.

On November 29th I was up early to sort the things in the trunk that Shou-yu had brought. Wally took the day off to help with decisions and preparations. About nine o'clock Professor March, an American teaching at some nearby school, came to say that all Americans were ordered out.

The Army would have a truck waiting for us at Erh Ch'iao the next morning.

Then it was a veritable tornado of packing and sorting. Wally went to find a carriage, but they were all hiding for fear of being commandeered by the military. He found one driver who was willing to hide his rickety cart in our yard until needed, and then take us to Erh Ch'iao for $2,200. Preposterous, but no help for it. In the end we paid him $2,500.

About midday we saw an amazing sight. Soldiers were striding purposefully in Indian file past our house and heading into the mountains. We couldn't believe that China had such soldiers: well fed, well clad, well equipped, in top condition, carrying their own food so they wouldn't have to rob the people, and obviously capable of thinking in their own heads. Who could they be? Where had they come from? Could they be the Generalissimo's own elite corps that had never been used against the Japanese? They didn't seem to fit that theory. Could they be—yes, they must be!—the troops that General Stilwell had trained in India. He had always said that Chinese would make superb soldiers if they were treated like human beings, but he had to take them out of the country to give them that chance.

Stilwell had just been thrown out of China by Chiang, after stubbornly refusing to yield control of the men he had trained. One of his last acts before being fired was to visit the Liuchow area and map out a defense for the region, which would include us. What more logical than that Chiang, with Stilwell gone, would use these troops in a desperate attempt to halt the Japanese advance that was making even Chungking jittery.

I'll never know the truth of the matter, but I'll never forget those impressive men.

We got on the way at three. The children and I were wedged among numerous bags and boxes, as the only way we could have money for the trip to America was to sell lots of things at inflated Chungking prices. The driver sat on the tongue of the cart. Tai Sao, who had decided to go to Chungking with us, set out to walk, and Wally and Shou-yu took turns on the bicycle.

We got to Erh Ch'iao at six-thirty. Major Sharp said we would have to go into Kweiyang for the night, as there was no place near there. Wally, being more savvy about possibilities, found us a place nearby.

We went down three steps to a place where coal balls were made. Peggy fell into a puddle of water and coal dust. Behind this place was a fair-sized room, fairly clean, having two trestle beds with straw pads, and a table between them with a vegetable oil lamp. There were three windows, looking out on a tumbling stream, over which our room was built like a bridge.

There was no food available, not even boiled water, as the fire had gone out for the night. Wally went out and found a vendor of t'ang yuan, little balls of glutinous rice with brown sugar in the middle, which most people love and I abominate. He brought the vendor in, and we each had a few bowls of the things and the water they were boiled in.

Then Wally took the bike and went into Kweiyang for the night, hoping to collect $20,000 that someone owed him, lest I be short of money on the trip.

Bobby was supposed to be shut up at home until Wally came back. But somehow he got out and was never seen again.

I spread the sheet over one bed in the hope of isolating any inhabitants in the straw, and arranged it so that we could sleep in one bed, Peggy and Sally toe to toe, and I beside them—an arrangement that would become familiar to us as we went on. One quilt would do for all. Rolled sweaters served as pillows. There was a cuspidor that could be used as a night pot.

It had been a warm, summer-like day, but during the night winter came, a frigid blast whistling down the valley and through the cracks around our windows. I pulled the quilt tight around us and wondered where I had packed the children's warm clothes.

In the morning Wally came with the money, and we went to the truck. The only other American was Professor March, but there were several Chinese who were employees of American organizations. Wally couldn't go because he was in charge of evacuating the university, but I arranged for Shou-yu to go to help with the children. There was no sign of Tai Sao, though I kept looking for her. I learned later that she had been outside the gate, not admitted to where we were, and had watched us leave. Then she walked back to Hua-ch'i and worked for Wally for some time longer.

The children and I shared the cab with the driver. Everyone else huddled in the back of the truck. At every stop Shou-yu ran up to empty the children's potty and ask whether we needed anything.

We didn't start until eleven. I asked Professor March what day it was. He said, "November 30th, Thanksgiving Day."

In recent weeks we had often seen groups of emaciated refugees from Changsha plodding over the land looking for a place to stop, and begging vegetables from my garden. I had explained to Peggy that these were refugees, not beggars, and that anyone could become a refugee. We ourselves might sometime have to run away. It was cause for thankfulness that when the time came we had a truck to ride in.

When the truck finally pulled out Peggy said, "Now we're really traveling."

"Yes, dear, we're really traveling."

"Now we're really refugees, aren't we?"

And with an ecstatic sigh she settled down to the adventure of being a refugee.

We spent the first night at Tsunyi, the second at Sungkan, and the third at Kikiang, and then we came to Chungking, which is a chapter by itself.

Chapter 29

Lodging in Chungking was extremely scarce, as it must be in a city that has been largely demolished, but Shou-yu had friends. He got an invitation for the children and me to stay in the Central Bank dormitory. Our room had minimal furniture, including a bed with a broken leg so that I had to pile two suitcases to hold it up.

Chungking was having one of its frequent water famines. When the water system was out of commission, water had to be carried great distances in buckets hanging from shoulder poles. We were allowed one teakettle of water a day, for drinking, washing ourselves, and washing the children's clothes. I couldn't even think of washing my own clothes. We went out for all meals, and got as much soup and tea as possible. I was happy to find a restaurant specializing in northern cuisine, which is not peppery.

After a few days of this I was startled to see a well-dressed woman come to my room. When she spoke I recognized Lulu Hwoo, who had been a student at St. Olaf when Wally, Shou-yu and John Liu were at Carleton. She and John had married, and produced several children as fast as the laws of nature permit. She was plumper than I remembered, but had the same sweet face. She took us to her home, where her children cheerfully doubled up to make room for us. It was a lively houseful.

I went to the Canadian Mission Hospital for a rabbit test, which confirmed my suspicion that I was pregnant. This would make a difference in the amount of U.S. money I would be allowed to buy at the official rate for travel home and a year's living. The amount was set at U.S. $5,600. If I stayed more than a year I could apply for more.

Most business in Chungking at that time was done by "auction shops," dealing in anything they could get. Very little new merchandise could come into the country. No one wanted to keep money, with the inflation such that money would spoil almost before it could be spent, so instead, people hoarded goods of any kind they could get their hands on. When they needed cash they took some item to an auction shop, where it was snatched up by someone who needed it. You could find almost anything in the shops if you kept looking.

The window displays often showed a strange sense of relative values. I remember a show window where a suit of woolen underwear held the central place of honor, while two beautiful fur coats were pushed down in the corners.

Shou-yu busied himself taking my things to the auction shops. A suit Wally didn't like sold for $40,000. Several cakes of Lux toilet soap, hoarded for years, sold for $600 each, which translated to U.S. $30 per cake. Other things sold at equally improbable prices. I soon had the means to buy my allotted U.S. $5,600.

After a few days Wally arrived. He said that the day we left, the Japanese, who had already reached Tushan, turned around and went back the way they came. Whether it was because of the stiff resistance they were meeting, or because winter came so suddenly and they had no warm clothes, we could only guess.

We didn't want to impose too long on Lulu's hospitality, so Wally arranged for us to go again into the building on White Elephant Street in which we had camped when we first came to Chungking in 1938. We seemed to be closing a circle of some kind.

It was early January, 1945, when we found our way through a Chungking winter fog to the airport on the river bottom. An old DC-4 was on the runway. I heard the pilot say we would have to climb to nine thousand feet to get out of the fog. The parting with Wally was emotional, but I was not sorry to leave the city where dogs bark if the sun comes out in winter.

The flight took us over the "Hump," the obstacle hurdled by all the vast American airlift into China for the past three years. Thanks to a recent victory on the ground in Burma, we had to go only to eighteen thousand feet without oxygen, instead of twenty-three thousand as had recently been necessary. Even so it was not comfortable. Seeing the Himalayas from that perspective gave no sense of grandeur. It was like looking at a picture in the *National Geographic Magazine*. We came down for food and fuel every four hours, at Kunming, Dinjan, and finally, at midnight, Calcutta.

We had known that lodging in Calcutta would be difficult, with missionaries and others pouring out of China by the hundreds. As I sat waiting to go through Customs at three in the morning, a young man I had met once in Kweiyang asked me whether I had a place to stay. He took me to a refugee camp for missionaries that had been set up in a big sports club of some kind. As I recall it, there were several hundred army cots set up so close together that you had to climb over the head or foot, and one cold water faucet for the lot. The details of the two days we spent there are mercifully blank in my mind. I remember only that Peggy and Sally were awfully good sports about it.

Then Irene Vincent, of IRC days, popped up and said, "I'm getting you out of here." She took us to the China Travel Service, which had taken over a fine old boarding house with a big garden in a part of town where there was a sea breeze in the evening. Irene, who had come before the crush, had a big room with a veranda, reminiscent of the imperial days, for herself and her baby, Jamini. For me she had managed to get a small room with a ceiling fan in a neat annex, built for servants' quarters, from which a covered gallery led to toilet and showers. This was our home for nearly half a year.

The place was full of Chinese trying to get to America. We had good meals and good company, but little hope. Ships were not taking civilians, or if now and then they did, pregnant women were strictly taboo.

As time grew short, Irene began working out a scheme for me to go and set up housekeeping near people she knew in Travancore until the baby was big enough to travel with. Before I took any decisive step, the word came that the U.S. government was going to charter the *Gripsholm*, the same ship that had been used for exchange of prisoners of war after Pearl Harbor, to clear out "all Americans born or unborn." It would also take the stranded Chinese, and pick up several hundred Americans who had been stuck in Greece during the war.

A month in a seaside hotel in Bombay, and a month aboard the *Gripsholm*, and I arrived in New York with Ricky still inside me. A doctor, certifying me for air travel, said, "You will probably make it, but the head is already engaged." The stewardess on the plane was warned that she might have to radio for an ambulance at any stop.

So at last we came to Granddaddy's house, the beacon of security that had sustained Peggy through all the uncertainties of the journey. Rick considerately gave me two weeks to get organized before he made the doctor sacrifice a day at the lake. He was born on August 19, 1945, just after the bombing of Hiroshima ushered in the Atomic Age, and ended the war against Japan.

When he was nearly three we rejoined his father in Shanghai and lived through the chaos leading up to the Communist take-over, but that's another story.

AFTERWORD

July, 1948. It was time to return to China, to be a family again if we were ever going to be. Rick, the baby who was born when we arrived in America, was two years old. Sally and Peggy were five and seven. It was time for them to know their father and their country. My husband, Wally, was teaching in Shanghai. I had hoarded enough of the money the Chinese government had allowed me to buy for the trip to pay our steamer fare. There was no reason not to go.

There was one sour note. During our long journey home, when we waited half a year in India for a ship that would take civilians, and I was at my wits' end, not knowing what to do about the coming baby, Granddaddy's house had been Peggy's beacon. The thought of it had sustained her through all the uncertainties, and there she had found a stability that she had never known in China during the war. It was bitter to be uprooted again. She regularly cried herself to sleep on the ship. She said she would not adapt to life in China. She would not learn the language, and so I would be forced to take her back to America to go to school.

Wally met us at the dock and took us to the home of his younger brother, Kelly, who lived in an apartment in what had been the Japanese concession with his pretty wife, Jane, and two-year-old daughter, Lili. They had squeezed in a bed for us and cots for the children in their living room. It would have to do until we could find our own place, which was not easy. The apartment was pleasant except for one peculiarly Japanese feature: the toilet was in the corner of the kitchen. Kelly had rigged a curtain around it, and everyone pretended that it was private, although we had to overcome a certain squeamishness.

The thing that impressed me first was the fantastic inflation that had occurred during my three years' absence. The $5,600 of American money that I had been allowed to buy for my trip home had cost only 112,000 *yuan* at the official rate, and would have been only 336,000 on the black market. Now it cost a million yuan to go a few blocks down the street in a pedicab.

Before I could master the vocabulary for dealing in such sums there was a currency reform. The new unit was to be stable, at four for

REMEMBERING CHINA 1935-1945

one U.S. dollar, because it would be based on gold. To provide the gold base, the government confiscated all the gold and silver in private hands. For years people had put all their savings into precious metals to escape the inflation. Now they must exchange their hoard for a handful of new, crisp banknotes. If people tried to hold some out, and their servants betrayed them, they were clapped into prison or even executed as an example. A newspaper reporter told of finding several of Shanghai's leading citizens crowded in a jail cell. There was no choice but to surrender one's savings, though no one believed that the new money would be worth anything.

Long lines formed at the Central Bank to hand over the precious metal. With the new money in hand people ran to spend it as quickly as possible for anything that would retain its value and could be sold readily later: a case of toothpaste or razor blades, half a dozen bicycles, tools, lipsticks, dried milk, anything that was durable, easy to store, and in constant demand.

Of course the merchants were reluctant to sell, but if they tried to hold back their stocks they were in the same trouble as those who tried to hold back gold. There was no escape from impoverishment.

Chiang Kai-shek sent his son, Chiang Ching-kuo, to be the economic administrator for Shanghai, to ensure that the regulations regarding the new currency would be enforced. His clout was such that, marvel of marvels, prices remained stable for some weeks. This was pleasant and novel, but no one believed it would last. The government still needed vast sums to pursue its war with the Communists in the north. It couldn't shake its old habit of printing whatever it needed.

Although Chiang Ching-kuo managed to keep Shanghai in line for quite a while, places with less powerful administrators began to slip. Farmers didn't like to bring their produce to Shanghai when they could get more for it anywhere else. Food became scarce. By running to stand in line wherever she heard of food for sale, a woman could usually get enough to feed her family, but unless she could spend her day that way they might go hungry. Jane's *amah* could usually scrounge enough for the family, but we did not feel that we should share it. We found our own way.

Wally was teaching and I was working for the United Nations. Neither of us had time to stand in food lines. Wally found on the black market a twenty-five pound tin of American Army ice cream powder. Near my office was the warehouse where ships bringing bananas from

Taiwan were unloaded. The bananas were ripe and must be sold. They could not be taken to another port. I would go on my lunch hour with a big bag and buy bananas.

You can live for a long time on bananas and milk, but you can't keep on liking it very long. I still don't really like bananas.

Prices began to slip, food returned to the market, and life returned to "normal," meaning constant, unbelievable inflation. The time came when inflation outpaced the printing press, and payday meant a cashier's check on the Central Bank for several hundred thousand *yuan* (impossible to cash or use) and a handful of fresh banknotes.

When I collected my last pay before leaving for America in April, 1949, I received two cashier's checks for half a million each, and I can't even remember what I did with them.

The inflation was the constant background music to everything we did in Shanghai, but we still had to meet the normal demands of daily life. Wally was teaching in a college whose name I forget, and I had to find something to do.

I had assumed that I could get a good job in one of the many American government organizations then active in Shanghai, and be paid on the American scale, munificent by Chinese standards. I found that none of them could hire me on that basis because I had not gone through FBI clearance before leaving the States. If they hired me it would have to be as "local staff" on the Chinese pay scale.

The American Information Service (if I have the name right) thought of an expedient. The American Library Association had sent a mountain of books and professional journals to rebuild the shattered libraries of Chinese colleges and universities. These had lain for three years in a warehouse because no one wanted the dirty job of distributing them. Someone hit on the idea of letting me a contract to do it, thus bypassing the FBI.

They gave me a staff consisting of a Chinese librarian, three workmen who knew a little English, and two carpenters who built shipping crates and the long tables we needed for sorting.

For several weeks I spent my days in a very hot and dusty warehouse as the intense summer heat began to wane. I don't think we had a fan. We just sweated as we parceled out literature and science materials for colleges, textbooks and journals for medical schools, and so forth, and sent them on their way to where they were so badly needed. The main office cooperated by letting us know where to send them, and how.

There was one problem they couldn't solve. We had all kinds of materials for West China Union University in Chengtu, Szechuan. We could send it to Chungking by boat, but there was no way beyond that. Having lived in Chungking for two years, I couldn't believe that there was not constant traffic between there and Chengtu. I told Wally the problem, and he told friends. He soon found someone whose father regularly brought some product from Chengtu to Chungking, often sending his trucks back empty. A quick telegram to the father brought a most courteous letter saying he would consider it an honor to carry the books to Chengtu without charge.

I had the brief and pleasant experience of being a hero in that office, as the Americans marveled at the operation of the Chinese bamboo network.

As the book sorting job would not last long, I began looking for other possibilities. The United Nations seemed the best bet, and Wally sent out feelers in that direction. One day I heard that someone from the United Nations had been looking for me to be a resettlement officer in the International Refugee Organization. I sprang into action, but, not finding me, they had already hired someone else. The only position open was as secretary to the finance officer of the IRO. I didn't feel qualified for that, as I thought being a secretary required all kinds of office skills that I lacked. They told me that my function would be drafting English letters and reports. This I could do.

My boss, Joseph Liao, spoke English very well and wrote fairly well, but few Chinese can write English without occasional alarming lapses. I remember only one time when I had to put my foot down to overrule his choice of words. In typing an elaborate budget he had drawn up, I dropped "pieces of" from "10,000 pieces of towels." In the second version he had put the word back. I dropped it again. He rushed over to me,

"Your native language! Why do you keep changing that?"

I said, "Are you going to take scissors and cut the towels in pieces, or give them whole towels?"

My salary was stated in U.S. dollars, but paid in *yuan* at the current rate. We didn't have to take all the money on payday, but could take a little at a time as needed. The paymaster didn't want us to take less than ten dollars at a time, as it made too much work for him. Even ten dollars was usually too much for the day's marketing, and any amount left over would spoil. Two or three people would take turns drawing ten dollars to share.

We had to make our request for pay by noon. It was paid at the noon rate and ready by three o'clock. Wally's schedule as a college professor was such that he could come to the office at three and spend the money at once. That way we lost only about twenty percent of the value. People who had to wait until quitting time lost more.

As time went on, the inflation became so preposterous that the government was forced to legitimize the possession of silver dollars. Wally could then run to buy silver, and it was no longer impossible to keep money overnight.

At that time the IRO was a heartbreakingly interesting place to work. As a resettlement officer I would have been in the thick of the problems, but even from where I sat it was a scene to remember.

Shanghai had long been the end of the line for refugees from everywhere: White Russians fleeing the revolution, people escaping from Siberia, or later from Hitler, or all the chaos of World War II in Europe, and all the refuse from all the world. Now it was easy to predict a Communist victory in the crazy war that followed the defeat of Japan. Thousands of people were desperate to get out of Shanghai to any country that would admit them. Our halls were crowded with frightened people, while we beseeched the countries of the world to accept them. We would get two visas to one country, half a dozen to another, and maybe one (for a specialized professional) to another. The visas could never make a dent in the number of applicants.

The only exception was Israel. Still struggling to get established, she offered to accept all Jews who wanted to come. We sent two (or was it three?) crowded charter shiploads, but we still had Jews who didn't want to go to Israel.

As a Communist victory loomed closer it was clear that the crowds could never get out the way we were doing it. The fall of Peiping (by this time it was referred to as Beijing) had left our sister office there feeding a crowd of refugees who could not get out. Were our applicants to face the same fate?

Somehow we found an abandoned U.S. Army base on Samar Island in the Philippines and got permission to use it for six months. We knew perfectly well that we could not get the people placed by that time, but we felt confident that, confronted with an insoluble problem, the Philippine government would not kick the them out. To Samar they went. I don't know how many shiploads, and I don't know how it all came out because by that time I was struggling with my own problems.

I don't remember how many weeks we stayed in Kelly's apartment. Eventually we found a place in a new building in a part of the Chinese city whose name I can't recall. The building had been constructed without the vapor barrier that it should have at the base of the wall, so the walls never really dried out, and were soon covered with mold, but at least it was our own space. Elder sister-in-law Phoebe sent us a manservant who had worked for her. Lao Chang was pleasant and reliable and a fairly good cook, struggling to meet our needs for food and boiled water with a little Primus stove. The children liked him, and we felt comfortable about leaving them with him while we went to work.

We had not seen fit to put them into a Chinese school, and we did not want to expose them to the atmosphere of the American school. An older cousin came to teach them at home and to help them learn Chinese. They were soon chattering happily with the neighbor children, while learning the elaborate dances with bouncing balls that the others performed with amazing skill.

Peggy, mindful of her resolve not to adjust to life in China, would never let Wally hear her speak Chinese, but with Lao Chang and the neighbors she was soon comfortable, dredging up from somewhere the fluency she had had at age three. Sally and Rick also picked the language up rapidly, and the cousin began to teach them to read.

We had Sunday trips to parks, and I remember a great afternoon of kite flying in a large open space near our house. The marvelous kite in the shape of a soaring hawk rose higher and higher. Wally sent the servant to buy more string three times as the dot in the sky became smaller. I don't know whether this was as exciting to the children as it was to him.

We knew early on that a Communist victory was inevitable. The corruption and stupidity of the government, and the constant problem of how to survive the inflation, inclined many people to welcome any change. I remember writing in a letter, "Perhaps the Communists will be better for everyone except people like me who attach great importance to freedom of the intellect."

We kept playing with different ideas for ourselves. We might go to Hong Kong, or the children and I could go to America and Wally join us when the immigration laws permitted, or we might try for Hawaii or Singapore. Our ideas fluctuated with the news from the war zone, and with rumors about conditions in the various possible refuge areas. We never really unpacked, but I constantly repacked to fit the latest plan.

I think it was in February that Wally had gone to Szechuan for some business deal on which he hoped to make a huge profit. Americans were urged to leave on a certain ship which might be our last chance to get away. I made reservations for the children and myself, and sent a telegram to Wally. An answering telegram said, "Don't leave now." I cancelled the reservations and hoped it was not a mistake. I remember the morning when I sat at my desk and heard the deep bellow of the evacuation ship's whistle as it pulled out. My mouth felt dry and my stomach hollow, and I felt a sense of abandonment, but only for a moment. Then life returned to its usual chaotic course. Wally returned and we continued replanning and repacking.

The American consulate called a meeting of all remaining nationals to explain the plans for final evacuation. When the time came there would be Jeeps with loud speakers going through the streets. We were promised at least two hours' notice. I packed again for America.

The details of the last days are fuzzy in my mind. There came a day when I went to the office to collect my last pay and resign. They gave me a Jeep and driver to get home, but as we approached the Garden Bridge traffic was at a standstill in every direction, and the road behind us was filling up. I got out to walk, telling the driver to get himself back to the office however he could. On foot I could make my way through the mess.

Americans had somehow been notified to meet the next day at a certain place. I took Wally to the consulate to try to arrange an emergency visa for him. The staff were very willing to help, but could not push it through fast enough. He would have to go on the quota, but being born and domiciled in China put him on the preference list, so he would not have long to wait. Later when he escaped to Hong Kong he lost his place on the preferred list, but by going to Taiwan he regained it—a fine example of the weirdness of our immigration laws. At that time the Chinese wife of an American man was admitted without question, but the Chinese husband of an American woman had to go through more hoops than a man with no connection at all.

As an American I might have risked staying when the Communists came, assuming I could get out later if I wished, but I could not be sure that the new regime would recognize the children's dual citizenship and let them go with me. I did not dare take a chance on that. By Chinese custom, children belong to the father's family.

My mother-in-law, on a recent visit to Shanghai, had said, "I'm glad you can save one of my sons. I just wish you could take them all."

I went with the children and a pile of luggage to the gathering place. We were served lunch from an army field kitchen, and taken on an LST (landing ship tanks) to the hospital ship *Repose* at Whangpoo. This was a lovely ship with all the most modern medical and surgical resources. We shared a large ward with twenty-five or thirty other women. When we asked where we were going the answer was, "Hong Kong, and then we don't know."

Two British gunboats on the Yangtze had been shelled and many sailors wounded. As the British had no hospital ship in the Far East at that time, we took their wounded to Hong Kong for them. When we got there, we refugees had to wait while an interminable line of stretchers went ashore.

We stayed in Hong Kong for five days, sleeping on board and going ashore by day. The British navy, to thank us for bringing their wounded, made us their guests for sightseeing and fun. They took us swimming at Repulse Bay, showed us the incredible Tiger Balm Palace, and generally did the honors.

After five days, as we steamed out of the harbor, we asked again where we were going. "Manila," was the reply. Reaching Manila after several days on calm, sunny seas, we were not allowed to go ashore. We were there only to take on fuel and head for Japan, several days to the north. What would we do after Japan? "We don't know. We'll turn you over to the Army."

When we approached Yokusuka, a gale was blowing, and the pilot would not try to take us into port. We lay outside the harbor for two days until the wind abated. We learned later that the first word the Army had of our coming was a phone call from the ship as we lay waiting to come in.

In contrast with the Navy's vagueness, the Army showed remarkable organization. They took us on buses to an officer's mess for lunch, and then to a large hall where they had assembled everyone we might have business with in Japan: consular officials, bank representatives, travel agents, employment agents, medical services—everyone we could possibly need.

A man was sent to put iron bands around boxes that had been too hastily packed and were coming apart.

An arrangement was made that all who wanted to could sail the next day on the *General Gordon,* with third class berths and first class meals and privileges. Those who refused this arrangement were on their own. I was thankful to accept it.

Women and children were put up for the night in a building at what was called a relocation center, a place where arriving soldiers stayed while awaiting assignment, and departing ones awaited transportation. Our building had been mopped in our honor, so hastily that the floor was still wet. We had to traverse a long exterior gallery to get to the bathroom, and when we did we were subject to a chorus of whistles and catcalls from the next building which, we learned, housed incorrigibles waiting to be shipped home. The next morning someone found out that fifteen guards with fixed bayonets were on duty around our building all night.

The next day, waiting at the wharf to go aboard the *General Gordon,* I had a problem. We had not been allowed to get any Japanese money, and if any provision had been made for buying postage stamps I had missed it. I wrote a note to let my father know we were coming, but had no way to mail it. I explained the problem to a friendly-looking Japanese woman, and she kindly promised to send it by air mail.

So Peggy had her wish and we were going back to Granddaddy's house, after only eight months in China. Wally would follow when the immigration laws permitted. It was took several months for Wally to join us, but for the children and me, that was the end of our China experience.

INDEX & TRANSLITERATION

Following is a conversion of Wade-Giles to Pinyin Romanization for place names and for people of general interest. Page references are given for important people.

PLACES

WADE-GILES	PINYON	WADE-GILES	PINYIN
Chefoo	Chifu	Lu K'ou Ch'iao	Lukouqiao
Changsha	Changsha	Nanking	Nanjing
Chengtu	Chengdu	Pailingmiao	Bailingmiao
Chungking	Chongqing	Paot'ou	Baotou
Erh Ch'iao	Erqiao	Peking (Peiping)	Beijing
Hankow	Hankou	P'uk'ou	Pukou
Hopei	Hebei	Suiyuan	Suiyuan
Hua-ch'i	Huaqi	T'ai erh ch'uang	Taierchuang
Kialing (river)	Jialing	Tientsin	Tianjin
Kikiang	Jijiang	Tsinan	Jinan
Kunming	Kunming	Tsinghua	Qinghua
Kuomintang (KMT)	Guomindang	Tsingtao	Qingdao
Kweichow	Guizhou	Tsunyi	Zunyi
Kweiyang	Guiyang	Yangtze	Yangzi
Kweilin	Guilin		

PEOPLE

WADE-GILES	PINYON	FOUND ON PAGE
Chang Tze-chung	Zhang Zizhung	*111, 112, 113*
Cheng K'ang-chi	Zheng Kangqi	*81, 110*
Chiang Kai-shek	Jiang Jieshi	*11, 24, 26, 50, 96, 109, 186*
Ch'u Djang	Chu Zhang	*47, 110, 111*
Fu Tso-yi	Fu Zaoyi	*19, 20*
Li Tsung-jen	Li Zhungren	*19*
Pai Chung-hsi	Bai Chongxi	*19*
Sheng K'e-fei	Sheng Kefei	*86, 92, 115, 117, 131*
Tai Li	Dai Li	*95, 99, 100*
Wan Chia-pao (Ts'ao Yu)	Wan Jiapao (Cao Yu)	*60, 62*
Wang Ching-wei	Wang Jingwei	*1, 149*

Fitch, George, Nanking YMCA		*57*
Johnson, Nelson, Ambassador		*41*
Luganetz, Ambassador		*65, 66*
Paxton, Hall		*40, 41*

ABOUT THE AUTHOR

Bea Exner Liu, now eighty-eight, has been writing all her life, but seldom got around to trying to publish anything. Born in Northfield, Minnesota, she graduated from Carleton College and spent ten years in China as the wife of a Chinese college professor. Bringing her children to Minnesota after the war, she worked at a variety of jobs to support them. Her book for children, *Little Wu and the Watermelons,* won two awards, and remained in print for fourteen years. In addition to this memoir, she has a novel about civilian life during the war, and has published stories and poems.